MOSES: THE MAK

The *Character and Charisma* series introduces us to people in the Bible and shows how their lives have much to teach us today. All the authors in the series use their communication skills to lead us through the biblical record and apply its encouragements and challenges to our lives today. Every volume contains an *Index of Life Issues* to enhance its usefulness in reference and application.

By the same author:
Friends of God
The Power to Persuade

CHARACTER AND CHARISMA SERIES

Moses
The Making of a
Leader

CLELAND THOM

KINGSWAY PUBLICATIONS
EASTBOURNE

First published 1996

ISBN 0 85476 537 9

Designed and produced by
Bookprint Creative Services
P.O. Box 827, BN21 3YJ, England for
KINGSWAY PUBLICATIONS LTD
Lottbridge Drove, Eastbourne, E. Sussex BN23 6NT.
Printed in Great Britain.

Acknowledgements

It is a shame that the cover of this book wasn't big enough to include the names of all the people who deserve to be there! Yes, I was the one who put pen to paper, but many others assisted in the process and without them, *Moses: The Making of a Leader* would never have seen the light of day.

My wife Rachael and boys Oliver, Barnaby and Jacob helped enormously by putting up with me sitting at the word processor or studying books for hours on end when I really should have been spending time with them. And our lovely friends, Martin and Debbie Harris and their children James and Lucy, were an enormous source of inspiration to me when I felt tempted to give up.

The Revd John Martin, of Word of his Grace Ministries, Essex, Jeff Lucas, a member of the oversight team of Revelation Church, Chichester, and Frank Prideaux, Pastor of New Life Church, Emsworth, all played an invaluable role by studying the text and putting me right on many areas of fact and theology. And Chester Tugwell used his literary skills to help when mine were not up to the task.

But my last thank you should go to two men who have been through God's leadership training programme and who lived to serve others for many years. Both are referred to later in this book, but deserve a special mention here. One is my father-in-law, John Barr, pastor of the Elim Pentecostal Church in Canning Town, and the other is Metcalfe Collier, one of the founding fathers of Brigadier Free Church in Enfield, who sadly passed away in October 1995. Both of these men of God have played priceless parts in helping me a little way along God's path for my own life. Without their love and commitment at different times, I simply wouldn't have made it.

Cleland Thom
Chichester 1996

Moses had an inspirational father-in-law. So have I. His name is John Barr and over the years he has been a pastor, counsellor, and friend to me. This book is dedicated to him . . . a real man of God.

Contents

Preface

The Bible isn't just the most inspiring book that's ever been written. It can also be one of the most frustrating.

Sometimes it describes people and events in the most intricate detail, and on other occasions it is strangely silent, leaving us to speculate on what might have happened.

It is these silences that cause problems in writing a book like this, which attempts to be both a biography and a commentary about the early part of Moses' life. Quite simply, Scripture misses out whole decades! For instance Exodus 2 jumps from Moses' boyhood to his manhood in less than a verse, telling us absolutely nothing about what happened in between.

In order to get around problems like this I must ask you to forgive me for doing two things.

First, I have inserted historical, geographical and cultural background throughout the book in order to bring colour and put 'flesh' on the Bible's factual 'bones'.

To do this I have referred to a number of books including *The Holy Land and the Bible* by Cunningham Geikie, *The Exodus Enigma* by Ian Wilson, *The Eyewitness Guide to*

Ancient Egypt, by George Hart, *Great Men of the Bible* by F. B. Meyer, *The Bedouin* by Volk de Wueste, *Egyptian Religion* by E. A. Wallis Budge, *Discovering the Biblical World* by Harry Thomas Frank and *A Way Through the Wilderness* by Jamie Buckingham.

I have also indulged in a little speculation here and there. For instance I have based my account of Moses' education, childhood and upbringing on the lifestyle which a boy like him would have experienced growing up in Pharaoh's courts. I have used a good deal of imagination in relating some of Moses' encounters with Jethro and describing his wedding. And I have taken a particular view on controversial issues like Zipporah's attitude to circumcision and Jethro's relationship with God.

I do not pretend that my imaginings and interpretations are always the right ones, but they are one way of looking at issues or events about which Scripture is silent. You may have your own views—I hope you have! What I have written is intended to both illustrate and stimulate.

I hope, though, that my embellishments will serve to make Moses' life more realistic so that we can learn from it. If they do, then perhaps they will have been excusable!

Introduction

The wind whipped at the walls of the big marquee, making them flap and balloon out wildly. It was a typical British summer's evening—cold and bleak.

A celebration meeting had finished an hour ago: two faith-filled hours of praise, worship and teaching. Now the marquee was almost empty apart from some people dismantling the PA equipment and a family sitting huddled together in a dimly-lit corner. I made my way towards them, wondering why I had been asked to counsel them. As I drew nearer, the scene told its own story . . . a husband and wife and three children aged between eight and fifteen, all sobbing uncontrollably, holding one another tightly for support, obviously unable to cope with the terrible emotional pain they were feeling.

I went and sat down with them and as I studied their faces my heart was filled with compassion. They looked broken, crushed and afraid . . . lonely, vulnerable and without hope. I wondered if they had been on the receiving end of physical and spiritual attack from an occult group, like a couple I'd counselled some years earlier who were in a similar state when I first met them.

I soon found out that I was wrong. Amid tears the family poured out their story. They weren't the victims of an occult group. They were victims of a church—a Christian church—where the treatment meted out to them by the leaders and other people was enough to make your hair stand on end. They had undergone three years of the most serious spiritual and emotional abuse. Their wills had been crossed, their characters assassinated, their relationships undermined, their ministries destroyed. Spiritual authority had been used to browbeat them and they had been labelled as rebels simply because they didn't do as they had been ordered. They had given up everything to serve the God they loved and had ended up with nothing. They had been treated like slaves—all in the name of a God who sent his Son to die so that his people could enjoy freedom.

My encounter with them shook me. I was the leader of a church myself at the time and after I left this family I went and had a good, long look at the way I handled God's people. I didn't like a lot of what I saw. How could I criticise the leaders who had treated this family so badly when in some ways I was just like them? I, too, had spoken harshly to people, had been unmerciful and unkind to them and had often failed to go an extra mile. I too had treated people's quite valid opinions as rebellious if they were different from mine. In other words, by God's standards I wasn't really qualified to lead. I hadn't completed— indeed I had scarcely started—his leadership training programme.

Sadly, the same can be said about many church leaders. The evidence is written all over their people's faces. There are so many good folk who have been crushed, mistreated, overlooked and treated unkindly in the frantic rush to see God's kingdom come.

Heavy-handed leadership is, of course, nothing new. A man called Moses was an independent hot-head who needed forty years of re-training by God before he was fit to lead God's people. When he began his ministry he was in some ways brilliantly trained and full of confidence. And yet because he had not been prepared by God he ended up with blood on his hands . . . and other people suffered as a result.

This book will explore how God trained Moses and made him into one of the greatest leaders the world has ever known. Perhaps as you read it you will recognise God's dealings in your life, too, as he prepares you for ministry, leadership or whatever he has in store for you.

My hope is that this book will help us to be people who are humble, who treat one another with tenderness and mercy and who lead through serving, not through lording it over one another or misusing God's authority.

After Moses died he was described as the meekest man who ever lived. If we allow God to train us like he did Moses, maybe they'll write something like that on our tombstones one day, too.

1

A Man of Destiny

The scene was horrifying: hundreds of near-naked men labouring in furnace-like temperatures, standing in deep, muddy clay pits making bricks. The air resounded with the fierce crack of rods and the awful screams of the slaves as grim-faced task masters lashed scorched and bleeding backs, driving the slaves harder, punishing every slight pause for rest and ruthlessly ignoring cries for mercy. Sweat poured from gaunt, emaciated bodies as the vicious midday sun hammered down on them from the unforgiving sky. Flies and other insects crawled across their faces and bodies, biting and stinging their flesh.

Slowly, torturously, some of the men used their chapped and bleeding hands to hack bundles of straw into small pieces, while others stood knee deep in pits, treading the chopped straw into the mud to create a thick, cement-like mixture. And then a few yards away yet more slaves slapped the mixture into row upon row of crude wooden frames and left them to dry. A few hours later the sun bricks, as they were called, would be baked hard and the slaves would turn them out and stack them in piles, ready

15

for use in houses and other buildings in the majestic cities of Pithom Tell er-Retabeh and Raamses Pi-Ra'amese, both set amid the black, fertile plains of the River Nile.

Some men were working with just one hand, the other limb hanging painfully at their side after being broken when fending off a blow from the rod.

Many of the slaves were racked with disease. Some were barely conscious, simply going through the motions of existence. And a fortunate few would find freedom that day . . . through anonymous, undignified and yet welcome death, from sickness, exhaustion, or through a beating. Many was the time when the Hebrew slaves risked punishment by casting their eyes longingly towards their homeland across Egypt's north eastern border . . . far away, and beyond all reach thanks to the crocodile-infested canal that ran along the frontier.

Both of the military cities, breathtaking in their magnificence, were primarily used to store treasure, along with supplies like wine, grain, meat and precious metal for the Pharaoh. The ruler then was Rameses II[1] who had already secured his place in Egyptian history by becoming the greatest builder his nation had ever known. He had used slave labour to build a capital in Egypt's Delta region for the first time in hundreds of years and a massive mortuary complex on the west bank of the Nile at Thebes. Each building was simply breathtaking . . . an architectural masterpiece, with ornate columns, pillars, ponds and intricately designed gardens. Fine monuments and statues, mainly of the narcissistic Rameses himself, stood everywhere. Each one was beautifully sculpted and colourfully decorated—one of them was seventeen metres square and weighed more than a thousand tons.

But the magnificence and the finery concealed a grim history. For Pharaoh's achievements during this time of unparalleled national influence, grandeur and luxury, were paid for with blood, and with shame. They were founded on brutality and cost the lives of the glorious people of promise.

It was a scene, then, of utmost depravity—one of history's darkest hours for God's people. And yet even Pharaoh, with all his might, his wealth and his wisdom, had not grasped one critical factor: that—like all things in the upside-down kingdom of El Elohe, God most high—the degradation and bloodshed he had inflicted were not producing death. Instead they were producing life as God exalted the humble, lifted up the downtrodden and fulfilled the promise which he had given Abraham centuries before to multiply his people. So as a result of God's faithfulness, the Israelites had grown in number and in influence. And the immortal Pharaoh Rameses II, who owned everything and everybody in Egypt and who was worshipped and revered as a god himself by his people, grew increasingly afraid.

A God of suffering?

Oppression. Bondage. Suffering. You could hardly describe the Israelites' existence in Egypt as the blessing of God—and it seems a contradiction in terms for God's people to be captives to anything or anybody. If God is a God of freedom, then ideally, his people should be free! So why were the Israelites forced to become slaves and endure such dreadful conditions in Egypt? God prophesied the period of captivity. He told Abram in Genesis 15:13: 'Know for certain that your descendants will be strangers in a country not their own and they will be enslaved and ill-treated for four hundred years.' But the loving God who is revealed to us throughout Scripture is certainly not one who sits in heaven and shoves humanity around some great cosmic chessboard at his own whim. God loves his people too much to play those kinds of games with them. Certainly there was a sense in which God used their suffering for good in order to prepare them for a future relationship with him which would be quite different from the idolatry they had grown up with in Egypt. It is also true to say that throughout the Bible, the idea of freedom for God's people is always measured in comparison with an earlier period of captivity—we are freed *from* something, *into* something. But to understand what was happening here, we need to turn the clock back more than 400 years—and to remember that God always has the best interests of his people at heart.

When famine hit the entire known world in the nineteenth century BC, Jacob and his household, who had always known God's plentiful provision, faced the prospect of imminent starvation. And we are told in Genesis 42:1, 'When Jacob learned that there was grain in Egypt, he said to his sons, "Why do you just keep looking at each other? . . . I have heard that there is grain in Egypt. Go down there and buy some for us, so that we may live and not die."

Now Jacob was right—there was corn in Egypt. Plenty of it, in fact, with merchants travelling from far and wide to buy it. And little did Jacob know it was his long-lost son Joseph who had been storing it there for the past seven years and who was now responsible for its administration. Egypt was the obvious place to go, and eventually the whole of Jacob's clan settled there, in Goshen, in the north eastern region of the Nile Delta. There they soon found that life was much easier than it had been among the tiring hills and valleys of Canaan. Their flocks thrived and so did they, especially with Joseph there to look after their interests.

Now Joseph had been taken to Egypt by Midianite merchants during a period when a Semitic people known as Hyksos had invaded and conquered the country. The fact that Joseph was a Semite, too, and that he came from the same geographical area as the Hyksos probably made it easier for Pharaoh to elevate him to the influential position of 'Prime Minister'. However, the Hyksos were finally expelled and the Egyptians later regarded foreign Semitic people, like Joseph's descendants, as both a military threat and a constant reminder of their former foreign rulers. So eventually the Semitic people—the Israelites—were taken into slavery.

You could hardly say it was the Israelites' fault that they became captives. And it is hard to see why God allowed such terrible circumstances to occur. But we need to see the situation from a wider perspective. God had three purposes in allowing his people to become slaves to the Egyptians.

1. He wanted to keep his promises

God promised Abraham that he would become the father of a nation. But his plan was threatened by the famine in Canaan. Had Abraham's grandson Jacob stayed there, both he and his family would have been wiped out. Joseph makes that clear in Genesis 45:5–8. So, by moving Jacob and his clan to Egypt, God was able to guarantee that his people were safe and that his promise to create a people of his own from Abraham's descendants still held good.

God used Egypt again as a sanctuary to keep his promises hundreds of years later when he told Joseph to take the baby Jesus there to avoid being slaughtered by King Herod. The geographic shift meant that Jesus escaped the massacre, and the life of the promised Messiah was preserved.

God is good at responding to changing and 'unforeseen' circumstances, mainly because he sees them long before anybody else does! As a result he sometimes has to allow us to go through periods of difficulty in order to achieve his wider purposes. Unforeseen circumstances are not on our agendas, but they are always on God's.

2. *God can bring good out of difficult circumstances*

If you look at life's circumstances through human eyes, it is sometimes easy to conclude that things are going hopelessly wrong. And in some ways they are! But thinking this way places a limit on God's ability to bring good out of everything, no matter how painful and difficult.

It might appear cruel, even wrong, that Joseph had to be sold into slavery by his brothers and then endure years of imprisonment in Egypt for something he did not do. But he was the catalyst in a chain of events which first led to the salvation of Joseph's father and brothers, and then eventually brought deliverance for millions of God's people.

We must learn to look at life's knocks from God's point of view. Yes, they hurt and are often desperately cruel and unfair. But alongside the pain are God's promises to bring healing and to use those circumstances to bring tremendous good . . . providing we are prepared to give him the time. Jesus' death on the cross is probably the best example of this. From a human point of view, it was a disaster: he was struck down in his prime and his ministry destroyed just three years after it began. But from God's point of view it was the only way to bring glory and resurrection life, not just to his Son, but to the rest of humanity, too.

3. *God loves to display his glory*

The Israelites' years of slavery were certainly difficult. But they none the less provided God with a wonderful opportunity to reveal himself as a great deliverer, and as a keeper of his promises. They gave him the chance to demonstrate his love and his power by performing incredible miracles. The plagues, the exodus, the parting of the Red Sea . . . none of these events would have taken place had the Israelites not been taken into captivity.

The death of my father hurt me more than anything I have ever lived through. But in a sense, it was worth the pain in order to discover new dimensions of God's tenderness, his ability to comfort and the blessing that he promises for those who mourn. Although some of life's circumstances can be bleak, seeing the way God redeems them and displays his love through them can make them worthwhile.

So while it was tough on the Israelites to be used as slaves in Egypt, the story did not end there. God had wider purposes in mind.

In a crude hut made of dried mud, straw and pebbles, a young Israelite woman lay on a tattered rug in the scorching afternoon heat. She was heavily pregnant . . . and equally heavy in heart. Tears poured down her cheeks, mingling with beads of perspiration. Another slave woman tried, vainly, to comfort her.

They had just heard the grim edict from the royal courts. Pharaoh had ordered the Hebrew midwives to kill all Israelite baby boys at birth because the Israelites were becoming too numerous, a threat to national security. In their hopelessness and fear, both women prostrated themselves on the dusty floor and called out to their God to raise up someone who could deliver them from their misery, captivity and pain.

A people in bondage

Right through history, God's people have never known freedom for long. No matter what God has done, they have unfailingly managed to get themselves into bondage of one sort or another, either to religion, sin, self-effort, worship of false gods, wrong doctrine or captivity by their enemies. God's freedom plan for humanity was sabotaged by man for the first time in the perfect environment of the Garden of Eden and the pattern has been repeating itself to this day.

Fortunately, however, God's mercy is everlasting and he always steps in and raises up a man or woman to bring hope, deliverance and judgement and to usher in yet another new era of his grace and love. These are people of destiny, people who know their place in history, people who are stamped with God's call right from conception and even earlier . . . people who understand that God made them what they are and created them for a life of good deeds, prepared in advance for them to do (Eph 2:10).

People of destiny

Jeremiah was one such. God told him that he had selected him to be a prophet to the nations before he was born. John the Baptist was another, conceived in impossibility and birthed in prophecy. And of course Moses was one of the greatest—a man born for a purpose . . . a purpose that probably burned in his heart from the day he was born to the day he died. As Stephen acknowledges in Acts 7:20, he was no ordinary man.

Gerald Coates, the leader of the Pioneer network of churches, often says that he was born for the 1990s. In other words he's saying that God's mission for his life is such that it simply couldn't have been slotted into any other generation. He knows his place in history.

So should we. We all need a captivating sense of destiny. We need to understand that all of our personal circumstances, including when we were born, where we were brought up, the things that have happened to us and the types of people we are, have all been sovereignly allowed by God to train us, develop us and to work his word into our hearts. We must realise that we are Christians because we have been chosen and raised up by God himself. Without this understanding—which can be exciting, sobering and frightening all at the same time—we will never hold out under pressure and we will lose sight of our vision, our calling and our goals. You were born for a time like this! History was waiting for your first cry after you left your mother's womb.

It waited for Moses', too, in the same way. For as the oppression of the Israelites became more relentless and cruel, they began to call on the name of their God. He responded by raising up his man.

The atmosphere in the *Per'ao*, Pharaoh's awesome stone palace, was tense. Pharaoh Rameses II frowned as he sat amid the grandeur and opulence of his throne room, his face clouded with anger. His courtiers and officials stood reverently around him, gazing nervously at the colourfully patterned tiled floor, unsure what to say.

The problem? A recurring one . . . the Hebrews. They were continuing to grow in number. The latest estimates put the Israelite population at around 600,000.

Nothing that Pharaoh had tried to do to solve the problem had worked. First he had ordered them to be taken as slaves. But even a grim and merciless regime of hard labour, forcing them to build cities and till the ground, had failed to slow down the birth rate. So then he had issued the order to midwives to kill all their baby boys at birth. But that did not have any effect, either—there were

Israelite baby boys everywhere. And so the threat to Egypt's security was becoming graver. Pharaoh feared that the Israelites might join forces with the Hittites or another enemy to fight against him. After all, his soldiers had been battling with the Hittites in Syria for years and had still not defeated them. Then, of course, there was the prospect of them returning to their own country. If that happened, Egypt would lose almost all its workforce and the building projects in Nubia would grind to a halt.

Pharaoh paused, turned to one of his servants. 'Are they here yet?' he demanded.

The servant nodded.

'Then go and get them.'

The servant scurried away and returned with Shiphrah and Puah, two of the Israelite midwives. They had been given their orders by Pharaoh several months earlier—to kill the Hebrew baby boys at birth. But they were both God-fearing women and had refused to go along with the grim edict. Now here they were, back before Pharaoh, ready to explain their rebellion and perhaps to pay for it with their own lives—for in Egypt, Pharaoh was the only one who could pass the death sentence.

The servant ushered the nervous women before the golden throne and they kissed the ground beneath Pharaoh's feet in the customary way. Their hearts quaked with fear as they looked at their ruler, who was wearing the ceremonial false beard, held in place by a band around his jaw, and a white double crown, with a sinister cobra's head mounted on the front.

Pharaoh's voice was quiet and yet full of menace. 'You know why you are here?' Both women were silent. 'I told you that you must kill all Israelite boys at birth. But it appears that you have been letting them live. If this is so, it is a serious act of rebellion against Pharaoh's authority.'

There was a pause and then Shiphrah broke the silence. 'The Hebrew women aren't like Egyptian women,' she began, hesitantly.

'That's right,' joined in Puah. 'They are very vigorous. They give birth easily and their babies are born before either of us gets there. That is why we have not been able to comply with your order.'

Both women stood and waited for Pharaoh's response. They had endured months of emotional turmoil, knowing that if they were to obey God in the situation they would have to disobey their ruler—and lie about it, as well. They had discussed what to say to Pharaoh many times, taking comfort in the fact that at least there was some element of truth in their story—Hebrew women *did* give birth quickly. Their hearts beat rapidly at the prospect of instant punishment. Pharaoh stared at them, almost with disinterest, thought for a while and then said, 'Then we'll have to deal with this situation another way, won't we? The growth of the Israelites must be stopped. They are becoming a danger to us.'

He turned to one of his senior officials. 'You are to issue a decree throughout the land. It must be declared in every province. You are to tell the people that every new-born Hebrew boy must be taken from its mother at birth and thrown into the River Nile. That will guarantee their death, no matter how quickly the mothers give birth.' The official stiffened with shock and the two midwives gasped.

'Yes!' declared Pharaoh, triumphantly. 'They must be thrown in the Nile. Let them drown! May the river flow with blood!'

Little did the Pharaoh know how true his words would eventually prove to be, or how bitter a harvest he would reap from what he was about to sow.

The scene was tranquil in the cool of the dawn. The silty waters of the River Nile shimmered and sparkled in the early morning sunlight and wild ducks and geese squawked loudly as they thrashed wildly across the surface. Palm trees swayed and rustled gently in the breeze and in the marshes and fields near the banks of the 4,000-mile river, some peasant farmers were picking vegetables and papyrus, which would later be used to make paper, sandals, rope and baskets. Further upstream two fishermen were guiding a wooden boat along with a long pole and a gang of men were using a shaduf (a trellis supporting a pole with a counterweight) to hoist water out of the river and pour it into a crude chute to irrigate the fields nearby by way of a series of ditches and channels. It was March now, and the floods, which began unfailingly on or around July 15 each year, had long since subsided, leaving farmers and slaves the tedious job of watering their crops by hand. As each day went by, measuring posts along the river showed that the water levels had dropped a little further, making their task even harder.

During the age of the Pharaohs, Egypt's geographical shape was said to resemble a flower. The Nile Valley formed the stem, the oasis of Faiyuum was the bud and the Delta the blossom, or the life. And the Nile, which passed through a richer variety of landscapes, cultures and people than any other river on earth, meant more to the Egyptians than just being the world's longest river. Quite simply, it was their blossom—their primary source of life. Without the river, which wound its majestic course from Ethiopia and Sudan in the south, through some terrible deserts to the Mediterranean in the north, the ancient civilisations of Egypt would never have existed. The mysterious dynasties of the Pharaohs would never have come to pass. For life without the river would not have been sustainable amid the savage red and stony wildernesses that dominated the rest of the country.

No wonder, then, that the Egyptians saw the river in
mystical, spiritual terms. Historically, they worshipped
the elements of nature that were stable, enduring and
reliable, like the rising of the sun, which led to the evolution of Atum, the sun god. And the Nile was a god, named
Hapi, who was thought to live in a cave at the source of
the river. To the Egyptian people, the Nile represented the
difference between plenty and famine, life and death. In a
good year, when the monsoon rains to the south in tropical
Africa were intense, Hapi would arrive and the river
would rise up to six feet and the flood waters would
spread gently and benignly across the valley and delta,
leaving a thick layer of fertile mud covering the fields.
Then there would be enough food such as dates, garlic,
wheat, barley, fruit and vegetables, to feed the whole
nation for a year—providing, of course, that the waters
receded quickly enough to give the crops time to grow.
But in a bad year, when the water levels were low, famine
would strike and death from starvation would be a very
real prospect for hundreds of dwellers.

Now, on this peaceful, sparkling day, the historic river
was witnessing more death.

The busy farmers froze as three Egyptian soldiers,
dressed in light linen tunics, sandals and carrying black
and white shields, spears and fearsome looking scimitars,
marched solemnly along the soggy river bank a few hundred yards away. One of them was carrying something: a
small bundle wrapped in cloth, a small bundle that was
crying. When the soldiers reached the water's edge the one
carrying the bundle unwrapped it, and took out a newly-
born baby boy, scarcely more than twelve hours old. His
defenceless naked body, wrinkled and pink, was in stark

contrast to the soldier's bronzed, rippling muscular frame.
His hoarse, insistent cries for his mother disturbed the
beautiful calm of the morning. Suddenly the soldier,
spurred on by his cheering comrades, swung his arms and
hurled the baby twenty feet into the river with a shout of
exclamation. A flock of birds took to the air, their squawks
drowning the final death cry. Then the baby's body gently
sank to the bottom of the river, to join scores of others.

Their duty done, the soldiers walked off, still laughing.
Maybe one hesitated, a tinge of regret clouding his mind
for a moment. And in a clay hut a little over a mile away, a
mother lifted her head and wailed.

The slaughter of the innocents

Satan's attack on humanity, and on infants in particular, is
nothing new. He has been determined to destroy life ever
since God spoke to him in the Garden of Eden after the
fall of human beings. God told him that he and humanity
would always be at odds with one another. Jesus didn't
refer to him as a murderer for nothing. That's exactly what
he is and the Jewish people, who bore the seed which
would eventually produce the Messiah, have always
been his special targets.

Satan got to work quickly after God had pronounced the
curse on him in the Garden of Eden. Adam and Eve had
not been out of the Garden for very long before the first
blood was spilt. Their eldest son Cain was so jealous of his
brother Abel that he killed him, despite receiving a personal warning from God that sin was crouching at his door,
ready to consume him.

The pattern continued throughout the Old Testament. In
the time of Queen Jezebel, countless Jewish people joined
in the evil worship of Baal by hurling their tiny babies into

the flickering flames of the sacrificial fires. And King Xerxes turned his wrath against the Jews in Esther 3:13. He issued an order that all of them—young and old, men, women, children—were to be killed on a specific day. They were to be slaughtered without mercy and their belongings taken away.

And then after Jesus was born, King Herod issued a decree almost identical to the one given by Pharaoh before the birth of Moses. He ordered that all boys under the age of two in the vicinity of Bethlehem be slaughtered in order to wipe out this newly-born King of the Jews. The bloodshed and grief must have been devastating.

God's warning to Joseph in a dream made sure that Herod's satanically inspired edict failed to achieve its object. But Satan still didn't give up. He was still determined to destroy God's promised Messiah. He had to, for Jesus' mission wasn't just to bring redemption to mankind, but to destroy Satan's works (1 Jn 3:8). The stakes were high: there would only be one winner. So Satan tried a different tactic, and through his ungodly inspiration began and maintained a chain of events which led to Jesus' death on the cross. How delighted Satan must have been when Jesus breathed his last. It had taken him centuries to get his man—but he achieved his goal in the end. Imagine how he must have felt later when he realised that under God's edict, first given after the murder of Abel, anybody who shed innocent blood had to pay for it with their own life . . . and that in killing Jesus, he had in fact signed his own death warrant. The words 'It is finished' (Jn 19:30) would haunt him for eternity.

Even though Satan knows his ultimate fate at the end of the age—he and his demons are destined to perish in the eternal fire (Rev 20:10)—his attack on humanity has not relented. He still opposes the gospel. He still kills, and it is still children who are among his primary victims. Maybe we're living in similar times now to those of Moses and Jesus, when Satan knew that God's deliverers had been born or were about to be born and went to any lengths to destroy them. Perhaps Satan knows now that the current generation is a significant one for God's end-time purposes on the earth and has sought to destroy them in any way he can. How many tens of thousands of lives have been coldly and deliberately ended in the abortion clinics across the world, their lives sacrificed on the twentieth-century altars of convenience, expediency and a woman's right to choose? Our methods of destruction might be more palatable on the face of it than the barbarism of the Baal worshippers. But the result is the same.

We need to be crying out to God for mercy over the whole issue of abortion right now. We will find, as the Egyptians found, that if you sow death, you reap it. Pharaoh sowed the deaths of the Israelite children, and paid for it with the death of his own son and all of his nation's firstborn. Without God's mercy our nation, and others, may find that there will be a terrible price to pay in the years to come.

Note

[1] There is some debate about which Pharaoh presided during the time of the Israelites' oppression and the subsequent Exodus. Exodus 1 gives us a significant clue. We are told that the Israelites were building the cities of Ra'amses and Pithom. Ra'amses was Egypt's Delta capital, named after and largely built by Ra'amses II (c.1290–1224 BC), superseding the work of his father Sethos. Ra'amses I only ruled for a year and does not really enter the equation. Before Sethos I and Ra'amses II, no Pharaoh had built a Delta capital since the Hyksos period (Joseph's day). So the city of Ra'amses is truly

an original work of these kings. So the Exodus must have fallen after 1300 BC, and probably after the accession of Ra'amses II in 1290 BC. However some scholars set the Exodus as being much earlier, in around 1440 BC, in which case the Pharaoh who 'did not know Joseph' would have been Thutmose (1539–1514 BC) and the Pharaoh at the time of the Exodus would have been Amenhotep II (1447–1421 BC). I have gone with the earlier theory, which is generally seen as being the more credible.

2

A Man with a Background

The young mother's fingers were white with strain as she wove the damp papyrus into the shape of a basket. 'Keep watch!' she whispered urgently to her two young children as they peered nervously out of the dimly-lit hut. 'You must keep watch! Look out for the soldiers!'

The woman's heart missed a beat as her baby, who had been asleep on a pile of rags on the floor, started to gurgle. She quickly put the half-made basket down on the ground and picked up the baby and cuddled him, placing her hand gently across his mouth and rocking him reassuringly. Already many of her friends had lost their baby sons as a result of Pharaoh's evil death sentence on new-born boys and the woman, a fine-looking Levite named Jochebed, had no intention of letting her handsome youngest son join the others at the bottom of the Nile.

The baby gradually became calm again and Jochebed put him down and resumed her basket-making, grabbing handfuls of warm pitch from a rough, stone jar and smearing it over the rushes to make them water-tight. As she did so her oldest child, a mischievous-looking girl named Miriam, jumped down from the window and wandered over to watch her.

'What are you doing? What's that for?' she asked, pointing to the basket.

'We're going to put your baby brother in it and place him in the river!' explained his mother. 'If we give our baby over to our God, then he will take care of him. You'll see.'

'How will he do that? He hasn't done anything to help all the other dead babies, has he?'

Jochebed sighed to herself. How could she explain such difficult concepts to little children? She had even found it hard to convince her husband Amram about her plan. But eventually he had managed to grasp her simple faith. 'We must remember Abraham,' she had told the man who was her nephew as well as her husband. 'Remember what happened to him with his son Isaac. If we give our baby over to El Elohe, the same as Abraham did with Isaac, then he will give him back to us. I know he will. He is faithful.'

For some reason the story of her forefather, which had been passed down by word of mouth by her family over lonely desert campfires for hundreds of years, had been burning strongly within her for weeks now, ever since her baby had been born. So gradually the plan took shape. They would place their baby in a basket and float it in the River Nile . . . not through fear or cowardice, but in faith. Faith that if they gave him to God, he would give him back to them. Faith that if they were prepared to sacrifice their own flesh and blood to the point of death, then he would honour them with life.

Anyway, any course of action would be better than the days and nights of terror that they had endured since the baby had been born . . . the hours of trying to stop him from crying when they heard the squads of soldiers marching round the slave colony, savagely seizing every newborn boy they could find . . . the stomach-knotting worry of being found out, or perhaps of being betrayed by some of their own people. Yes, anything would be better than that. Amram and Jochebed had done everything they could to preserve this baby, this gift from God. They could not keep their secret any longer. He was getting too big and too noisy, and they had to face the fact that sooner or later he would be discovered. They simply had to do something before the soldiers found him . . . and trust the God of Abraham to do the rest.

The royal procession made its way grandly up the banks of the Nile, with several slaves carrying Pharaoh's daughter aloft on a golden chair mounted on long poles. The water lapped coolly against the river's banks and the palm trees rustled softly in the breeze. Eventually the procession came to a suitable spot for bathing and the chair was placed carefully on the damp grass. The Princess was slender and pretty, with large dark eyes and short cropped hair covered by a headdress and a wig made of the finest quality hair. She was dressed in a fashionable, delicately pleated robe which was folded round the waist, with the two top corners pulled over her shoulders and knotted under her breasts to keep it in place. Around her shoulders was a glistening, colourful collar made of gold rings which had been intricately threaded onto twine along with beautiful stones—orange-red carnelians, green feldspars and mauve amethysts. Her body was adorned with silver and gold amulets and jewellery and her eyes were lined with black kohl. There was rouge on her cheeks and red lipstick on her lips. Fine red leather sandals covered her feet.

The Princess was eager to bathe in the cool waters of the Nile and then return to her palace where servants would later massage her body with precious oils and creams and apply more make-up and perfume.

The Princess's Syrian maids, wearing gaily coloured embroidered dresses, led their royal charge up the banks towards the water, clearing a path for her to paddle in as they went.

'Wait!'

The maids stopped and turned to the Princess and looked at her inquiringly, wondering what she wanted.

'What's that?' The Princess pointed to a spot a few yards along the river. Yes, there was something floating past.

'Go and get it.'

Two of the Princess's maids removed their sandals, hoisted up their dresses and waded through the murky water until they reached the basket. In their curiosity they didn't notice Miriam's dark, shining eyes watching the scene breathlessly from behind some bulrushes close by. One of the maids bent down and picked up the basket and carried it back to the Princess. It was heavier than she had expected. The other attendants gathered round, chattering animatedly and wondering what was inside. They didn't have to wait until the lid was lifted to find out. A sudden cry from inside the basket told its own story. The Princess quickly pulled back the lid and looked at the robust baby boy inside. His arms and legs were flailing furiously and he was obviously frightened by the strange surroundings and by the crowd of unfamiliar faces.

She laughed in surprise and then picked the baby up and studied him carefully. The baby's features and complexion were certainly not those of an Egyptian. She thought for a moment and then gradually began to understand what was going on. She noticed the slaves' huts a short distance away and remembered her father's command that all new-born Hebrew boys be killed. Emotion suddenly welled up inside her and she felt sorry for the baby. Her eyes filled with tears.

'Why, this is one of the Hebrew babies,' she said to her maids. The girls looked embarrassed, unsure of how to react. Would the Princess go along with her father's edict? What would she do—throw him in the river or hand him over to the soldiers to do it?

Suddenly there was a rustling of bulrushes and Miriam, unable to control herself any longer, burst out eagerly, much to the astonishment of the royal party. She found it hard to get her words out in her excitement. Maybe her little brother would be safe after all! 'Shall I go and get one of the Hebrew women to nurse the baby for you?' she gasped.

Pharaoh's daughter looked at Miriam with amusement. 'Where did you come from, little girl?' she asked, and then thought for a moment. 'Yes, go and get her.' Miriam scurried up the bank towards her mother's hut as fast as her legs could carry her.

A few minutes later she returned with Jochebed, whose face was looking taut and white with fear. She bowed low before the Princess, fighting off the maternal urge to grab her baby back and cuddle him safely. Then she looked up slowly and her eyes met those of the Princess, who smiled at her reassuringly.

'Take this baby and nurse him for me,' said the Princess. 'I will pay you.'

She handed the wriggling baby back to Jochebed, who hugged him closely to her as though she would never let him go. 'Thank you,' she breathed. 'Thank you.' As she turned to go, her eyes met the Princess's again . . . and lingered briefly. The Princess held her gaze. It was a look that conveyed a secret that these two women would keep for ever.

Jochebed and Miriam ran back towards their hut clutching the baby, their hearts bursting with joy. God had done it! They'd given their baby to him—and he had given him back, just as they had prayed he would. And not just that, but now they could keep him, confident in the knowledge that the Pharaoh's daughter had guaranteed his safety—*and* had agreed to provide enough money to pay for his upkeep. How ironic—Pharaoh supplying the money to pay for the upkeep of the man who might turn out to destroy him! God certainly has a sense of humour.

Later that day Amram and Jochebed knelt and cried prayers of thanks to their God, with Jochebed still clasping the bewildered, struggling baby to her bosom. And in the grandeur of her palace, Pharaoh's daughter sat alone and thought . . . and wondered exactly why she had done what she did . . . and what her father would think about it when he eventually found out, as he surely must.

Jochebed looked around nervously as she followed a servant through the halls of Pharaoh's palace with her child, now a sturdy little boy, by her side. Ornate columns, each inlaid with green, blue and red glazes and gold, towered over her. Ominous statues of gods and animals made of different coloured stones stood against the brightly painted walls. Beneath Jochebed's feet, spectacular coloured pictures of plants and birds adorned the floor.

The servant led her into the royal court where a party was in full swing. Her nose wrinkled as she inhaled the strongly perfumed air. Dozens of revellers were gorging themselves on grilled meat, bread and fruit, drinking copious amounts of wine and groping and teasing one another without any kind of inhibition or shame whatso-ever. There was laughter and cheering and the hall thronged with the sound of music from a small orches-tra. There was a riot of movement and colour as two dozen seductive, near naked dancing girls moved to the pulsating beat, entertaining Pharaoh's leering guests. The little boy drew closer to his mother and clasped her hand fearfully, unable to comprehend the unfamiliar surroundings.

Jochebed was ushered before Pharaoh's daughter, who was relaxing on a divan and eating grapes and figs from a stone bowl while chatting animatedly to some of her ladies in waiting. She paused and looked up at Jochebed, who bowed low.

'He's a fine boy, isn't he?' said the Princess, looking at his bronzed face and sturdy body. Jochebed nodded, unable to speak through emotion. 'Well, he will be safe here,' said the Princess, ruffling his black hair. 'He will receive the finest education there is. He will be taught by the finest scholars in the kingdom. He will be trained to be a soldier—a leader of men. He will be a Prince in the royal court and will want for nothing. You can be sure of that. He is fortunate to be able to leave the slave colonies.'

Jochebed nodded again and bravely gulped back the tears, feeling as though her heart was being pierced with a sharp sword. She walked up to her son and hugged him, kissing his smooth brown skin repeatedly, tears now streaming down her face and onto her tattered brown cloak.

'You must stay here now,' she whispered to the boy. 'This lady will take care of you. No questions now,' went on Jochebed firmly, as the boy looked into her eyes. 'You must stay here. It will be for the best. The God of Abra-ham will protect you and keep you. His face will always shine upon you and he will give you his peace. Goodbye, my child.'

Jochebed thrust her son towards his new mother and then turned round and walked away with her head held high, allowing herself just one last, fleeting glance at the boy she would probably never see again. Then she turned away again, a firm and controlled action, and then ran out of the palace into the dark, empty streets, sobbing bitterly and uncontrollably. And yet amid the bleakness of her pain, the presence of her God was strangely and reassuringly close. Once again she had given her son to him in faith—and knew without doubt that he would look after him.

Families—God's choice

There's an old saying that goes, 'You can choose your friends, but you can't choose your family.' And it's true. We have no say whatsoever on the people who are likely to be the most significant influences on our lives. We are formed from them and they are thrust upon us—for better or worse. And whether we love them, hate them, honour them or reject them, the fact is that they are still our parents—and always will be. There's nothing we can do to change it.

That's why it is so important for us to remember that although *we* had no say in who our parents were, *God* certainly did. And we can be confident in the fact that he picked the right people for the job, even though they might have failed us, rejected us or even hurt and abused us. We can see right through Scripture how God chose particular people to parent certain children. Jesus is the obvious example—Mary and Joseph certainly weren't a random selection! And neither were Zechariah and Elizabeth, the parents of his cousin John the Baptist. They were particular people, with a particular job to do. This knowledge can help us to honour our parents—even when they don't deserve it.

The same applied to Moses. His parents, Amram and Jochebed, were hand-picked by God to give one of the greatest men in history the right start in life. Even though their roles as parents only lasted for perhaps a few years before they handed their infant son over to be cared for by Pharaoh's daughter in the royal courts, the fact remains that they had a crucial role in preparing him for a fascinating, demanding and often dangerous life ahead.

Amram and Jochebed were both members of the tribe of Levi—descendants of Levi, one of Jacob's murderous sons who was roundly cursed by his father on his death bed (Gen 49:7) for his bloodthirsty ways. Maybe that's where Moses got his murderous tendency from later on in life. Perhaps it was an ancestral problem. We can't say for sure. We only have to look at our own families to see how characteristics—and sins—can be passed down the family line from generation to generation.

Amram was fifth in line after Abraham and belonged to the clan of Kohath. He lived to be 137—seventeen years longer than Moses. The names of both of Moses' parents are significant. Amram meant 'people exalted' and Jochebed meant 'divine splendour' or 'Jehovah my glory'. These names conveyed the fact that they knew the God of their forefathers personally. And perhaps their names also give us prophetic glimpses about their son Moses, who would later be used by God to exalt his people after hundreds of years of captivity and radiate God's splendour to such an extent that people would be afraid to look at him.

Amram and Jochebed were both born into slavery in Egypt and would have lived through the grim oppression of Pharaoh's rule. The names they chose for their first two children, Miriam and Aaron, provide clues to their suffering. Miriam is a derivative of Mary, which means 'bitterness'—a good word to describe the miserable lot of the Jewish people. And Aaron means 'woe to this pregnancy'—a real cry, if ever there was one, from the heart of this weary slave girl.

The Bible doesn't disclose much about Moses' early years. He may not have been named until he was older, for there is some uncertainty as to who named him and when. He may have had another name while he was young. And we don't know how long he remained with Amram and Jochebed. All we are told in Exodus 2 is that he was returned to Pharaoh's daughter when he was older.

However it is reasonable to assume that he remained with his parents for long enough to learn some of the truths which would provide a bedrock of belief for the whole of his future. He saw the suffering of his people and of his father in particular as he returned home, exhausted and covered in blood each night after working long days making sun bricks or working in the fields. Who knows what burdens about justice and freedom God was placing in his heart even then?

Amram and Jochebed must have prepared him for the time when he left them and his older brother and sister to go and live as a Prince in Pharaoh's courts. The prospect of having their son grow up amid the immorality and spiritual wickedness of the palace would have certainly provided them with an enormous spur to bring him up in God's ways while they had the chance. They surely learned the lesson that a wise writer of Proverbs (22:6) discovered later . . . 'Train a child in the way he should go, and when he is old he will not turn from it.'

The same applies to all of us who are parents rearing children in a society where they may well be exposed to many kinds of sin, occult practices and vice by the time they reach their mid-teens. If we provide them with the correct foundation of truth and love and a knowledge of their heritage in God while they are young, they will be able (if willing) to withstand even the worst kind of batterings and temptations when they are older . . . because a house genuinely built on the Rock never falls, even though it will certainly be buffeted occasionally.

Moses must have known about his tribe, the Levites, and about his clan, the Kohathites. He probably heard stories about his people's history, of God's dealings with Abram, Isaac, Jacob, Esau and Joseph . . . about their struggles and difficulties . . . and of course, about the unceasing blessing of this strange God who stood anonymous and unparalleled in ancient civilisations which were ridden with idolatry. But the boy is unlikely to have merely received head knowledge of this God. He probably received something of God's love into his heart . . . a revelation which would later prove to be strong enough to withstand years of contrary teaching and evil influence of Egyptian priests, magicians, philosophers and scholars.

And he must also have often wondered why his mother sometimes held him close to her and wept, not really understanding that the day when she would have to abandon him to the care of another was growing dauntingly closer.

Families—a mixed blessing

Although Moses had every reason to be grateful to his parents for the good start they gave him in life, his brother and sister, Miriam and Aaron, were a mixed blessing! You could hardly call them wholehearted followers of God. While Miriam certainly developed into a prophetess of some ability, she eventually became so jealous of Moses that she and Aaron both spoke out against him and were afflicted by leprosy as a result. Similarly, although Aaron became Moses' spokesman and right hand man and was the first High Priest, he was also responsible for getting the whole Jewish nation to worship a golden calf while his younger brother was up Mount Sinai receiving the Ten Commandments, including the one which explicitly forbade idolatry! Hardly a brother and sister to be proud of! Like most of the rest of the people of their generation, they found it difficult to follow God wholeheartedly. On good days, they would be strong in their relationship with him. But when things got tough, they wavered and floundered. Although they followed God out of slavery, they never had the resolve to follow him into anything else. No wonder they never entered the Promised Land! According to the New Testament they were double-minded—and unstable in all they did (Jas 1:8).

So Moses probably found his family a mixed blessing— just as we do sometimes! Yet he always remained loyal to them. When God expressed his intention of wiping out Aaron, Miriam and the rest of his people for worshipping Aaron's golden calf, Moses pleaded with him to save them. And when God afflicted Miriam with leprosy he again prevailed on him to heal her. No matter how great his work for God became, or how significant a man he was, he never forgot his roots or his family ties, even though they weren't perfect and were often a hindrance to him. Neither should we. They are a crucial part of God's training programme for our lives—if only we can set aside our hurts and preconceptions and see God's wider purposes at work. Quite simply, our families are an essential ingredient in our formation as leaders and effective Christians—even if they might not appear to have been at first glance.

If you look at the lives of most of the people who were significant for God in Scripture, you'll find in almost every instance that their family circumstances weren't ideal. Who would want a manipulator like Isaac's wife Rebekah for a mother—or a deceiver and a schemer like Jacob for a father? Who would want a villainous bunch of brothers like Joseph's—men who were so jealous of him that they stripped him, threw him down a well and left him to die, and then went home and lied to their father about what had happened? We should be encouraged to learn that power struggles, feuds, jealousy and even violence are nothing new within families—even families who are trying to honour God and walk in his ways. These things started when Cain killed Abel and have been continuing ever since. And yet within all the wrongdoing we can see God's hand at work if we look hard enough. It is always there, reaching into the middle of our family crises, if only we can take the time and have the courage to see it. That's what Joseph did. Although he had every reason to hold resentment against his murderous brothers, he was still able to say to them in Genesis 50:20, 'You intended to harm me, but God intended it for good.' That's what we must learn to believe, even in the most difficult family situations. If we aspire to be God's leaders, or want to be really effective for him, one thing is for certain—we will have to come to terms with our family upbringing at some point. If we don't it will be a ghost that is always there to haunt us and it will affect the way we serve others. This process may mean confronting the agony of divorce, the shame of sexual abuse, the pain of repeated broken promises or the wounds inflicted by our parents' harsh tongues. But we must allow God and his people to heal us so that we can be free to use the past as an opportunity to help people rather than allowing it to be an obstacle. We must see that God is using our suffering to serve his wider purposes—and that he works all things together for the good of those who love him if only we will give him the chance.

What's in a name?

There is some debate as to who gave Moses his name. Was it his mother, Jochebed, or was it Pharaoh's daughter? Scripture is not clear—and there is evidence to support both views.

In Exodus 2:10 we are told: 'When the child grew older she [Jochebed] took him to Pharaoh's daughter and he became her son. She named him Moses saying: "Because I drew him out of the water."' The problem with this passage is—which 'she' named him? It is difficult to say for certain—and in fact, both women may have played a part in the decision!

Many commentators believe that 'she' was Pharaoh's daughter and that she chose the name because the Egyptian word for 'child' or 'one born' was *mase*, which is pronounced quite like Moses.

However, you cannot get away from the fact that the Hebrew name 'Moseh' means 'to draw forth', a Hebrew play on words on the fact that he had been drawn out of the water which would not have been obvious to an Egyptian. So this tends to lend weight to the argument that Moses was actually named by his natural mother and that his Hebrew name *Moseh* was assimilated into the Egyptian royal court as *Mase* (child, or one born). But whichever way you look at it, there is no doubt that Moses' name gives us a clear prophetic glimpse about his future role as the one who drew God's people forth—out of Egypt, through the waters of the Red Sea.

Names were often very important in Bible times. Sometimes, as with Moses, they were used to commemorate a significant occasion or circumstance. In a previous generation Abraham and Sarah laughed their heads off when they were told that Sarah would get pregnant in her old age . . . and they later decided to call their surprise package 'Isaac', which is the Hebrew word for 'he laughs' or 'laughter'. And when Isaac's wife Rebekah had twins, she called the second one Jacob (Hebrew for 'he clutched' or 'he clutches') because he was born clutching his brother Esau's heel. And the illustration went even further, for the Hebrew term 'to take by the heel' also means 'to overtake' . . . which is exactly what Jacob did to Esau when he tricked Isaac into giving him the family birthright.

People's names often acted as a prophetic signpost, too, indicating the kind of ministry they would have when they were older. It's not clear whether the parents were aware of the fact when they chose the name. Maybe they were— or maybe they were like many people nowadays and just fancied the name! But you can't deny that the links between the names and the ministries were often very powerful. Who can deny that Isaiah (which means 'Yahweh is salvation') wasn't a fitting description of a man who wrote more richly and prolifically about the coming Saviour than anybody else? And there is a clear link between Amos (which means 'burden bearer') and his ministry which bore God's burdens to see righteousness, justice and morality established among his people.

And then, of course, there were the people whose names were changed, either by God, or they changed them themselves. It didn't happen very often, but when it did, there were very good reasons. A change of name normally indicated a new chapter in the person's life. Abram (which means 'The Father is exalted') became Abraham ('Father of a multitude') and after that he became a new man with a new vision, a new destiny and a new promise of God on his life.

A man named Reuel (which means 'Friend of God') eventually became Jethro, which means 'excellence', or 'preeminence'—and, as we shall see, became Moses' father-in-law and the man who trained him for his role as leader of the Israelites. And Jesus changed the fearful and irrational Simon's name to Peter (Rock) to indicate the kind of role he would have in the New Testament church.

Hundreds of years later in the twentieth century, names are sometimes significant in pointing towards God's plans and purposes for our lives. Many Christians pray earnestly for God's wisdom before naming their children. However, important as this is, it is vital that we do not lose sight of the fact that who we are in *character* is far more significant to God than who we are in *name*. He will be far happier because we are joyful than because we bear the name Joy! And nowadays God does not often change our names when he uses us to fulfil his purposes. He changes our characters, our hearts, our thinking and our lifestyles instead. That is surely far more important.

God's training school

Moses is a living example of how God trains us from birth. But because God's ways aren't ours, it's easy to misinterpret what he's doing—or even miss it completely and give up through disillusionment. I have found through many years of counselling that people can cope with most difficulties provided that they can understand what God is doing in their lives at the time. And in most circumstances, he is training them!

Our training methods these days tend to place a strong emphasis on courses, teachers, mentors and diplomas, and these things are not necessarily wrong in themselves—in fact our churches would be a lot poorer without them. Then there is the secular training we receive at schools, colleges, universities and other centres of learning. Education, and the people who administer it to us, has an important part to play in shaping our characters and our thinking, making us the people we are and perhaps preparing us for our future ministries.

However, God's training programme is generally very unconventional and a great deal less pleasant! We don't formally enrol, and we certainly don't get a diploma to say that we've completed the course. For his training school usually involves suffering, pain, wounding and rejection.

To our way of thinking, the last way of training someone to be a leader of God's people would be to have them handed over to be looked after by the very people who had already killed hundreds of children like him. Who can quantify the pain and confusion that Moses must have suffered as he left the loving confines of his family to go and live in the royal palace? Orphaned. Rejected. Abandoned. And yet safe in the hands of his God. Strange ways to prepare someone for service. Strange—and yet effective, for God has the ability to use the awful circumstances which we all shy away from to soften our hearts and to reveal his love to us. To miss out on the circumstances would be to miss out on the facets of his character that we discover during them.

I remember once saying to God: 'Do whatever it takes to soften my heart.' Within twenty-four hours, our baby son, then four months old, was at death's door, fighting for his life with meningitis. My wife and I were given special counselling and told to expect the worst. Even if he lived, we were told, he would probably be brain damaged, blind or deaf. How he survived, only God knows. And during a two-week vigil by his hospital bedside my heart nearly broke a thousand times as I helplessly watched him in his pain and suffering during his struggle to survive. Yes, God softened my heart—and used some of the most awful emotional pain to do it. During those dark hours in the hospital ward he met me and my wife Rachael with the most unimaginable tenderness—and brought complete healing to our son. It hurt. But it was worth it. We met God in a new way—and have never been the same since. And now we have a healthy, lively six-year-old as a testimony to God's goodness.

All of us need to keep God's training programme well in focus as we learn to cope with life's bitter blows. It couldn't have been more bitter for Moses. And yet look at the history-changing events that resulted from his wounds. The same will come from ours provided we do not become resentful but seek to understand what God is up to and allow him to form our characters in the fire.

3

A Man Prepared

The teacher was angry. He glared at the teenage boy sitting dolefully on the ground in front of him and then lashed him several times across his bare back with a thick wooden rod. The boy tried hard not to cry as the teacher shouted, scolding him for his laziness. The rest of the boys in the class kept their heads down and busied themselves with their writing, terrified that they would be the next victim.

Among them was a handsome fourteen-year-old whose features were slightly different from those of the rest of his class. But it wasn't just his looks which set him apart. He had a sense of authority and confidence about him which made him stand out from his peers. His name was Moses. And he wasn't just enduring the strict, often brutal Egyptian educational regime. He was also being trained by God, during what you could call the silent years.

The silent years

God's leadership training programme almost invariably involves a time when he works on us in private . . .

when he strips us of our props and our pretences, removes us from the crowd and puts us in his crucible where we can get to know him as a true friend. It's just us and him— and these times can be painful, lonely, and very tough. But they can also be times of great intimacy, when our relationship with God is established at a very deep level. It's like the stones used to build the temple in 1 Kings 6:7, which were worked on in silence away from the building site. Sometimes God needs to deal with us quietly and alone, so that we can become properly shaped living stones in the church (1 Pet 2:5), with some of our rough edges rubbed off. It's only when we are alone with our Creator that we can see ourselves as we really are—and see him as he really is. It's sobering. It's daunting. But it's the only way to true growth and maturity.

A married couple need to establish a relationship once the rosy glow of the honeymoon has faded a little. Their love and commitment for each other are not in doubt—but getting to know each other can take a lifetime, and can sometimes be very painful. Their love must be worked out in the day-to-day humdrum of life and be tested through hardship. And it's a process that just involves the two of them. Other people might be able to help with guidance and opinions. But at the end of the day they can't make the relationship work.

Many great men and women in the Bible went through the silent years with God. And because of the sheer intimacy of the work that he was doing in their lives, the Scriptures reveal very little about what went on. All we read about is the finished product. The rest is simply too personal to record.

That's why we know nothing reliable about what happened to Jesus between the age of twelve, when he got lost on his trip to Jerusalem, and the age of thirty, when he was baptised in public by John the Baptist. All the Scriptures tell us is that Jesus grew . . . 'in wisdom and stature and in favour with God and men' (Lk 2:52). We can only speculate about how that growth was achieved. He spent his formative years working as a carpenter in his father's workshop—but who knows about the craftsmanship that his heavenly Father was quietly achieving in his life at the time? Whatever it involved, we know that Jesus emerged from those silent years totally equipped for the pressures, temptations, successes and battles that lay ahead.

Samuel, John the Baptist, Moses and many other men and women in Scripture all went through their silent years with God . . . and we'll have to wait until we get to heaven to find out just what happened. Moses vanishes out of the book of Exodus for almost forty years. In chapter 2 we leap from his boyhood in verse 10 to his adulthood in verse 11 without so much as a pause for breath! What happened in between is almost a complete mystery. But during those years, God was laying vital foundations in his life and character which began to shape his thinking, his actions and his reactions. And although God does not give us the privilege of knowing what went on, it is possible to build up a general impression.

It is certain that Moses was brought up as Pharaoh's grandson—a Prince in the royal palace. Although it's unlikely that he was in line for the throne—the succession did not normally pass to foreigners or adopted children—he none the less had an exalted position and enjoyed the privileges and luxuries that went with it. Ladies from the royal court, including Pharaoh's daughter, his adopted mother, probably supervised a whole range of activities aimed at preparing him for his future years as a ruler in the New Kingdom of Egypt.

Formal education for boys like him usually lasted around ten years. When he was old enough he probably went to one of the colleges that centred around the Temple of the Sun—a bit like the Oxford, Cambridge or Harvard of Ancient Egypt. One such college was called The House of Life. Although we don't know for certain whether Moses went there, he certainly went to one like it along with the children of other nobles and members of the royal family. There they would have had a personal tutor, probably a high official or a retired military officer who was close to Pharaoh.

The education for young Egyptian men was strict—they were made to work very hard. The Egyptians were enthusiastic believers in a severe regime, with liberal doses of corporal punishment. Perhaps Moses read the advice given to youthful scribes, recorded on papyrus and discovered centuries later: 'O scribe, do not be idle . . . or you shall be cursed straight away. Do not give your heart to pleasure or you shall fail. Do not spend a day of idleness or you shall be beaten. A boy's ear is on his back and he listens when he is beaten . . .' (Papyrus Anastasi).

He probably spent long hours learning to read by chanting with the other boys, and memorising the complexities of hieroglyphics, using a reed brush and red and black paint to copy out ancient works which he didn't understand, daubing the picture-signs on wooden writing boards until he was proficient enough to use the more expensive papyrus. There would also have been rigorous, almost barbaric physical and military training at the hands of retired soldiers and instructors, and education by the priests in the Egyptian religions. Worship of the various gods was an essential part of the Egyptian way of life.

There were plenty to choose from. There was the sun god, named Atum, who according to one story, emerged standing on an earthy mound from amid the watery chaos at the beginning of time. According to Egyptian legend, Atum created the gods of the air and moisture, whose daughter Nut was the sky goddess. Her husband—who was also her brother—was called Geb and was the earth-god. He and Nut apparently had four children, Osiris, Seth, Isis and Nephthys, about whom there were many myths. Osiris was the god of the underworld—the dead king. He was also a god of vegetation and he introduced agriculture and wine making into the country. He was called the 'good being' or 'perfect one' and was one of the best-loved gods. Different stories about these gods represented the struggle between good and evil.

Another god, closely associated with the king, was Amun, the god of Thebes, who ultimately became the supreme state god. He was identified with another sun-god Re as Amun-Re. Then there was Ptah, the local god of Memphis, who was the patron of craftsmen, his wife, Sekhmet, the war goddess, Hathor, the goddess of love and music, and Ma'at, the goddess of truth, law and order.

Despite this proliferation of gods, however, it is likely that Moses was taught to worship Atum the sun god. He probably went to pay homage to him in a grand cult temple, built on the site where the god was supposed to dwell. The temple was situated on a large, lush estate and would have housed a treasury containing vast wealth. There were rooms containing linen for clothes and oils for anointing, and a library where sacred writings were stored. Brightly coloured paintings adorned the walls and there was an open roof so that the sun could shine in.

The temple was a place of great purity: it was kept isolated from the ordinary world and was enclosed by a high wall. Inside, a Chief Priest, acting on Pharaoh's behalf, performed diligent rituals in the temple sanctuary. Three times a day he and a number of lesser priests approached the god's shrine, accompanied by burning incense and lamps, scattering purified water from the temple's sacred lake as they went. In order to be ritually clean he and the other priests washed themselves in the sacred lake, shaved all over and dressed themselves in white linen robes. As the Chief Priest drew near to the shrine he would say, 'I am the pure one,' break a clay seal on the door and open it to reveal the statue of the god. He then washed the statue, anointed it with sacred oil, dressed it and made an offering of food before leaving the sanctuary with the other priests, with someone sweeping the floor as they went out in order to prevent any traces of their presence being left behind.

The Pharaoh was believed to be the gods' son on earth and it was his duty to feed and protect the gods and keep everything in order for them. When he did so it was believed the gods' *ka* (spirit) would be awakened so that its power could be used to preserve the country's order and harmony.

The ordinary people were not allowed into the magnificent temple. Only the priests and members of the royal family could enter, and Moses was probably among them. Ordinary folk had statues of gods in their homes and offered prayers and gifts in small local shrines. The only time they got a glimpse of their god was during one of several festivals held during the year, when the statue was paraded around the temple walls on a golden platform, accompanied by the Pharaoh, the priests and nobles like Moses. These festivals were magnificent holiday occasions and coincided with important events like the harvest or the flooding of the Nile.

Atum was described as 'the god besides whom there is no other' . . . a description almost identical to the one given to the God of Abraham whom Moses probably learned about during his early years being brought up by his real parents among the Israelites. Maybe the similarity between the two made it easier for him to comprehend the reality of a one true God later on. It's hard to say for sure. But there is clear evidence that by the time of the New Kingdom, Egypt had moved towards the idea of having one supreme god figure rather than the mass of national and local gods which had dominated previous centuries. Who knows, maybe Moses remembered the intimate friendship that his father and mother enjoyed with their invisible God and yearned to worship someone who was real rather than a statue . . . a god who was loving and just and who wanted to gather a people to himself and call them his sons and daughters. Maybe he yearned to speak to him face to face, as a man speaks to a friend.

All we can be sure about is that, during those silent years, Moses was being trained by God. And his training was probably the complete opposite to anything that his parents would ideally have chosen. Perhaps Amram and Jochebed were often racked with guilt over the way they had allowed their son to be exposed to false gods, the occult and the wisdom of other religions . . . the same feelings we wrestle with when we allow our own children to listen to ungodly philosophies at school and to mix with people who are a bad influence on them. But no doubt they found, as we do, that God's ways are not our ways and that he was able to use Moses' experiences to prepare him for the time when he would need all his skills to become the founder of a new nation state.

There's plenty of encouragement here for those of us who were tainted by the occult and other religious beliefs before we became Christians. Although there is nothing about these beliefs and practices that are acceptable to God, he can none the less use them for our good and for his.

The Bible (Acts 7:22) gives us three clues to the qualities which God put into Moses' life during those silent years. He was mighty in word. He was mighty in deed. And he was learned in the wisdom of the Egyptians.

What do these phrases mean? As a man who was mighty in word, he would probably have been a great statesman— a ruler and a politician. Pharaoh had many officials who helped him to govern Egypt, and the most important positions were usually held by family members. These officials helped to administer a strong and efficient system of government, collect taxes, deal with foreign trade, carry out foreign policy and to build up reserves of food for the years when the flood levels were low—exactly as Moses' ancestor Joseph had done four hundred years earlier. We can only guess what kind of role Moses had in the government of the New Kingdom of Egypt. Some historians think he played a major part in masterminding the massive building projects which characterised his nation at that point in history. But whatever he did, it must have been a task of great national importance. And it appears that he was successful enough to pose such a threat to national security that Pharaoh was swift to sign a death warrant on his own adopted grandson when circumstances merited it later on.

As someone who was mighty in deed, Moses was probably a great soldier—some believe he was a charioteer. The historian Josephus tells us that while Moses was still a young man, the Ethiopians invaded Egypt from the south and routed the Egyptian army which had been sent to fight them. The Ethiopians then advanced and eventually threatened the key Egyptian city of Memphis. A significant defeat, with the grim prospect of a total surrender, looked possible. But the Pharaoh's wise men recommended that Moses be appointed to lead a counter-attack. He took command of the dejected royal troops and surprised the enemy, driving them back to their homeland and even going as far as capturing their principal city of Meroe. The story goes that he later returned to Egypt to a hero's welcome, laden with the gold, riches, slaves and other spoils of victory.

So as a successful statesman and soldier, most of the key positions of state would have been open to him by the time God altered the course of his life again when he was forty. The world, at that point, was literally at his feet.

What about the wisdom of the Egyptians? What did it involve? This wisdom was a complex system of belief that was inseparably bound up with the Egyptians' religion. The Egyptians believed that human beings consisted of several parts: the *ka*, or spiritual double, created at birth and released from the body at death—similar to what we would call the human spirit; the *ba*, or soul, and the *akh*, or supernatural power. As long as the body was preserved, the *ka* and *ba* would live. This is why it was thought to be so important for a dead person to be properly mummified and laid in a tomb, where offerings of food could be made which would nourish the *ka*. Dead kings were preserved in pyramids so that their *ka*, or spirit, could benefit the country in the future.

As a result of this belief, most Egyptians were very preoccupied with thoughts about life beyond the grave. They would make meticulous plans for tombs to be carved out of rocks on a nearby hillside and furnished according to the customs of their country.

A belief in the gods was central to the Egyptians' thinking. And although there were many gods, as we have said already, the Egyptians' belief in a single god figure can be traced far back into history. Indeed, there was never a time when they were without this belief. The earliest Egyptian manuscripts talk of a god referred to as *neter* (since there is no 'e' in the Egyptian language, the vowel is inserted to make the word pronounceable). This god-figure was represented in the form of a large stone axe head, set in a wooden handle. If you bear in mind that in these prehistoric times, the mightiest man was the one with the largest axe, you can appreciate the significance of this symbol.

It is not clear what the word *neter* meant. It could have meant 'strength' or 'power', 'renewal' or 'renovation' . . . in other words a powerful god-being who could renew himself perpetually.

Ancient documents refer to this god as a creator of heaven and earth . . . as one who was pure, wise and merciful, who was there at the beginning of time and who was eternal. He was self-existent, immortal, invisible. And although there were numerous family gods and gods over cities, the Egyptians saw no contradiction in having these alongside one supreme god. As mentioned earlier we also know that they believed in an afterlife and in judgement for the dead.

No one really knows where these beliefs originated. But they were contained in a host of literature, hymns and prayers dating back to at least 3300 BC. Some of the writings contained moral guidance, some of the literature was in the form of beautiful poetry—and much of it was similar in some ways to the Bible. And we know for a fact that Moses became well versed in it all. When Acts 7 says he was 'learned' in the wisdom of the Egyptians, the word is the Greek word *paideuo*, which means 'to educate, instruct'— even to the extent of instruction by chastisement. So he knew his subject well—and perhaps his deep understanding of those ancient Egyptian manuscripts equipped him to write the first five books of the Bible later on. Certainly, there are some similarities in approach and style.

Thus there are some striking similarities between Egyptian religion and the God of Abraham. But having said that, it has to be said that the wisdom of the Egyptians also involved selfishness, idolatry, sexual immorality, magic and other occult practices—all things condemned by God. Personal morality did not really feature in it to any great extent. And so the similarities are deceptive—and dangerous.

The snare of deception

It's as easy nowadays to blur the wisdom of God with the wisdom of other religions and philosophies—especially with New Age beliefs running rampant right now. The similarities between their beliefs and ours are as close now as they were in the time of ancient Egypt. Some of the terms are exactly the same—I remember chatting to a New Ager in the street and he agreed with almost every term I used as I told him about my faith. But actually our beliefs were as far apart as heaven is from hell. The reality is that such doctrines and philosophies are simply the enemy's way of ensnaring us and deceiving us. That's why we need to be firmly rooted in the Bible—and in its author. The book of James expresses it well (3:13): 'Who is wise and understanding among you? Let him show it by his good life, by deeds done in the humility that comes from wisdom. But if you harbour bitter envy and selfish ambition in your hearts, do not boast about it or deny the truth. Such "wisdom" does not come down from heaven but is earthly, unspiritual, of the devil. . . . But the wisdom that comes from heaven is first of all pure; then peace-loving, considerate, submissive, full of mercy and good fruit, impartial and sincere.'

One of Satan's main tactics against the church is deception and we need to be very clear on the fundamental differences between other religions and Christianity. We cannot afford to make compromises—or excuses, even when pressured to do so in the name of ecumenism and tolerance. As it says in 2 Corinthians 6:14: 'For what do righteousness and wickedness have in common? Or what fellowship can light have with darkness? What harmony is there between Christ and Belial? What does a believer have in common with an unbeliever? What agreement is there between the temple of God and idols?' We need to understand that if we as Christians refuse to separate ourselves from evil, we will eventually lose our fellowship with God and our rights as his children. Moses had to renounce the wisdom of the Egyptians in order to be of any real use to God: he ultimately emphasised the differences by putting hundreds of his kinsmen to death for worshipping a golden calf while he was up on Mount Sinai with God. We need to be equally clear. And the only way to achieve this is to be rooted in Scripture— even, or especially, in this exciting age of the Holy Spirit. There is a desire to be radical nowadays—but the most radical thing we can ever do is obey the Scriptures as they were written rather than come up with new ideas that have at best a flimsy scriptural basis.

Powerful in word. Powerful in deed. Learned in the wisdom of the Egyptians. This was Moses, the man who emerged from his silent years with God. And although he must have been as familiar with that wisdom as the Egyptians themselves, these beliefs certainly did not capture him or shake his simple, boyhood faith in God. Quite the reverse—they left him determined to return to his roots, to his people, to his God. Why? Simply because information can never replace revelation. Knowing *about* other beliefs will never compare with the utter reality of knowing God.

The cost of knowing God

It is really knowing God, as a Father, a Friend, that the silent years are all about. Maybe you're in *your* silent years with God right now, a time when God is working in your life deeply, perhaps through difficult personal circumstances and trials. You find you are very much alone and that few people are able to understand what's going on. You probably don't understand much of it yourself! But during this time you need to remember that God has brought you to this season of quietness and loneliness so that he can establish a deeper friendship with you. There's nothing threatening about it—he's not out to get you. Only good will come of it. No one will ever know how he accomplished it. But as with Moses, everyone will notice the fruit that comes from your life afterwards. And you'll be glad for ever that you went through it.

Several hundred miles away, the sun disappeared behind the wadis and dunes in the waste desert places of Midian and darkness began to fall over a small Midianite settlement. There was silence apart from the bleating of sheep and goats, the howling of wild animals and the animated chatter of some men around a camp fire. An old man in his seventies stirred the embers of the fire with a stick and gathered his cloak tight around himself to keep out the piercing desert wind under the starry skies. Little did Jethro, a Midianite priest and prince, know that he, too, was about to emerge from his silent years. Soon he would meet another descendant of Abraham in an encounter which would change the course of human history for ever.

4

A Man with a Burden

Moses woke up with a start. The sunshine was already
streaming through the window of his room in Pharaoh's
palace, casting long panels of light across the ornate
furniture. Moses sat up and rubbed the sleep from his
eyes. Yes, that sick feeling was still there in the pit of
his stomach, just the same as it had been for weeks now. It
was there as he struggled to get to sleep each night, his
mind a turmoil of rampant thoughts. And it was there each
morning when he woke up after another restless night.

His conscience was troubled.

Moses climbed out of his sumptuous bed and rang a bell
for a servant, who arrived within seconds, bowed, and
proceeded to help his master wash and put on his royal
robes. Moses looked at the finery with a scarcely concealed
contempt and shook his head. Yes, his mind was made up.
No longer could he bear the hypocrisy of living the life of
an Egyptian in the luxurious royal palaces, when he knew
deep inside that he was an Israelite. It just wasn't right.
Yes, there were plenty of other Hebrews living and working in the palaces . . . people who considered themselves

fortunate to get the chance to exchange the oppression of the slave colonies for a life of service in the royal courts. But for him, it was wrong.

There had been plenty of occasions when he had sat in his chariot and watched his countrymen, his brothers, sweating and dying on the grim building sites, suffering under the sadistic lash of the slave drivers' rod and whips. And every time Moses saw them, he always had that nagging feeling that he should be there alongside them rather than climbing the social hierarchy in Pharaoh's palace. The situation had troubled him for weeks. But now he had decided it was time to act. Enough was enough. He would go back to his people—and lead them into freedom. No longer would he be known as the Hebrew Prince, the son of Pharaoh's daughter. He would be Moses—the deliverer of God's people! He had the strength. He had the ability—he had been trained by the best army commanders in the land. He had all the qualities of a leader. He would even be mistreated alongside the Israelites, if that's what it took to become their hero, the one who led them out of captivity and back into their own land beyond the River Jordan in Canaan. Yes, the time was right. Even though the cost was enormous and he stood to lose everything, it was the right thing to do. And as Moses finally made up his mind, he noticed that the sick feeling suddenly wasn't there any more. For the first time in a long time, he regained his peace of mind.

Choosing to go God's way

So why on earth did he do it? Why did an heir to the daughter of a rich and powerful monarch turn away from wealth, success and the prospects of greatness in order to become a slave? One thing is for certain—Moses wasn't forced into his decision or backed into a corner. Hebrews 11:24–27 makes it clear that he chose his course of action, carefully and deliberately. In other words, he weighed up the options and decided that he would actually *prefer* to go back to his people, in the full knowledge that he would face trials, punishment and oppression. The passage tells us: 'By faith Moses, when he had grown up, refused to be known as the son of Pharaoh's daughter. He chose to be ill-treated along with the people of God rather than to enjoy the pleasures of sin for a short time. He regarded disgrace for the sake of Christ as of greater value than the treasures of Egypt, because he was looking ahead to his reward. By faith he left Egypt, not fearing the king's anger; he persevered because he saw him who is invisible.'

The truth is that Moses faced the same choice we do. We either go our own way, which is usually easier and more comfortable, or we go God's, which is risky and full of the unknown. And the decision is not just one we take when we become Christians, but one which we face repeatedly right up until the time we die, just as Jesus did in the Garden of Gethsemane. We are all the sum total of the decisions we have made—or failed to make—in our adult lives so far.

The sacrifices involved in Moses' case were huge, the risks enormous and the cost high. The whole venture could have blown up in his face—and indeed, in some ways it did. But the passage from Hebrews indicates that there were several factors which helped him to make his decision. We can learn from them.

1. The deceptiveness of sin

First, he realised that sin is only enjoyable for a short time. Now we don't know for certain how deeply Moses was affected by the immorality and idolatry of the royal courts by the time he got to forty. It's comfortable for us to conclude that he led a clean and moral lifestyle, because such a concept fits more easily into our Christian idea of what a biblical man of God should be like! The truth is, we simply don't know. And indeed, if Moses *did* manage to maintain his morality within the royal courts, he was without question the exception rather than the rule. I personally think it's unlikely that he lived a terribly sinful lifestyle, but whether he did or not, he certainly came to a place where he knew that there was no way he could remain in the palace and follow God at the same time. It was one or the other. And he chose to go God's way because he realised that the good life would not last for ever.

Worldly pleasures always fade in the end. They're nice while they last—but there is always a price to pay later on. I always laugh when I hear preachers say how unenjoyable sin is! I've always found it to be quite the reverse—like those cream cakes, naughty but nice! It's the consequences—the guilt and the separation from God and from his people that are unenjoyable. And fortunately, Moses was wise enough to understand that there are more important things in life than enjoying yourself. Yes, remaining in Pharaoh's court would have been pleasant and challenging and would certainly have represented the easy option. But the pleasure wouldn't last for long. Going God's way might at first glance be harder—but in the long term, it always turns out to be the better option.

2. Long-term rewards

Moses knew that he would be rewarded if he chose to go God's way. But what were the rewards that made the prospects of fame and fortune in Egypt pale into insignificance? I don't believe that Moses was expecting any kind of reward on earth. There would have been few prospects of pleasure, wealth or honour in going back to his country-

men—quite the reverse! Had he wanted these things, he
would have remained where he was in the royal palace.
No, I believe Moses somehow had a clear understanding
and expectation of a reward waiting for him in eternity if
he was obedient to God. 'He persevered because he saw
him who is invisible' (Heb 11:27).

We should have the same. We live in days where we are
encouraged to enjoy the benefits of God's kingdom here
and now, on earth—and quite right, too. Jesus prayed
'Your kingdom come, your will be done, *on earth*, as it
is in heaven.' He doesn't just want us to enjoy 'pie in the
sky when we die' but 'steak on a plate while we wait'! The
kingdom of God is there to be experienced and enjoyed
here and now, not just in the future. But within all this we
should always have our eyes primarily fixed on the goal of
seeing God and worshipping him face to face in heaven
one day. Why? Simply because it's the only thing that we
can reliably put our hope in while we live on earth. It's the
only thing that won't let us down. For while it's not wrong
to put hope in answered prayers, prophetic words, good
relationships and dreams about the future, these things are
not always reliable, and can leave us very disappointed if
they don't work out the way we planned. But hope in a
reward of spending eternity with Jesus is guaranteed and is
infallible, and should be one of our main sources of
motivation in the Christian life. Other things, in comparison, are not that important.

3. Seeing the invisible

Moses had glimpsed the invisible God of the Israelites.
This sounds a bit of a contradiction in terms . . . he 'saw
him who is invisible' . . . a bit like hearing some silence!
What does this mean? Perhaps Moses had actually been
through an encounter with God, similar to the ones later

on, where he saw his back from behind a cleft in the rock and met him amid the clouds on the slopes of Mount Sinai. But perhaps it was simply that Moses was so completely and unswervingly sure that God would look after him and sustain him that it was just as if God had taken him to one side and had a face-to-face talk to him about it. After all, this is the whole nature of faith which the writer of Hebrews tells us in Hebrews 11:1—being so certain about things we haven't seen that it's as if we've actually seen them! And this is the sort of faith we should all aspire to: rock solid certainty, even if we look around and see circumstances that seem to suggest the opposite of what we're believing for. Although faith never denies the facts, it should certainly rule them. If we're penniless and trusting God for money, sick and trusting him for healing, or are single and hanging on for a partner, then we should be so completely sure that he will answer our prayers that it's as if he'd met us face to face and given us a personal assurance about it. That's when the *rhema* word comes in—the 'now-word' into the situation, the Bible verse or prophecy that sparks something in our hearts and gives us that certain knowledge that God is on our case. That's Moses-style faith in action . . . actually being able to see our invisible God. And it was this faith, together with the realisation of the folly of sin and the prospect of future reward, that enabled Moses to arrive at the decision that would shape history.

Later that day, Moses strode through the palace courts and went down to the stables, virtually ignoring the courtiers and officials who bowed to him gracefully as he walked by.

He commanded a servant to get his chariot ready and then jumped in and rode away from the palace towards a slave colony several miles away. When he arrived he reined in his snorting horses and stopped to watch the sickening scene, growing increasingly angry inside as he saw the people—his people—in their agony and shame. He sat silently for a while, and then suddenly he could control himself no longer. He leapt down from his chariot with his eyes blazing and his jaw set. A few yards away a cruel, swarthy slave driver was standing above a frail Hebrew man who had collapsed in the heat, thrashing him repeatedly with a short stick, his back a pulp of blood and flesh. The slave driver nodded briefly at Moses, laughed obscenities at his victim and then resumed his gory, sadistic task. Blood spilled to the ground and the man's shrieks drowned the weary cries of his countrymen a short distance away.

Moses quickly glanced about him. The coast was clear! Without warning he drew his long-bladed sword from its sheath, leapt at the slave driver and stabbed him in the back with one swift, fatal blow. The man collapsed to the ground, dead. The slave looked at Moses in utter bewilderment. 'Quickly! Run over there and get back to work,' Moses said, pointing to a group of men chopping pieces of straw a short distance away. The man scrambled up from the ground and ran off, his back still bleeding and his legs unsteady.

Moses glanced around again. Everything was going as planned. No one had seen what he'd done. He urgently dug a hole in the ground and buried the Egyptian slave driver, covering him up with sand and rocks. Then he jumped back in his chariot and rode home, his face grimly triumphant at the thought of a job well done. Yes! He would be the deliverer of the Hebrew people. Surely God had marked him out for the job since birth. He would kill their oppressors! The prospect of real power and influence made the adrenalin pump through his veins as he rode his chariot back to the palace, whipping the horses to make them go faster. Yes! The future was his!

The following day Moses awoke, not with a troubled conscience, but glowing with the feeling of elation. The future was his! What better way to show his commitment to the Hebrew people than to kill for them? How impressed they'd be—and how grateful! Surely now they would turn to him as their leader. Moses hurriedly dressed and thought what to do next. He would go back to the slaves to receive their adulation. He'd start to rally some troops. He would leave the royal palace and become a leader of his own people, the Israelites.

An hour later he stopped his chariot near the scene of the previous day's killing. Nearby, a wretched Hebrew slave stood drinking thirstily from a water bottle. Another slave came up and grabbed the bottle from him. 'Come on! Share that water! It's for all of us,' he snarled. The first slave pulled the bottle away and lashed out . . . and within seconds the two men were brawling on the ground.

Moses ran over and separated them. 'Why are you hitting your fellow Hebrew?' he asked the man who'd snatched the bottle.

The man turned to him and looked at him with contempt. 'Who made you ruler and judge over us?' he demanded. 'Are you thinking of killing me as you killed the Egyptian?' Both men laughed, turned their backs on Moses, and walked off together, their differences apparently resolved at the arrival of a common enemy.

Moses stood alone, dumbfounded, with the slave's words still ringing incomprehensibly in his ears. He'd been rejected by his own countrymen. Suddenly he was afraid. 'What I did must have become known,' he thought, his mind racing. His confidence, his plans and his dreams evaporated in the midday heat. He felt numb inside—and desperately afraid. He jumped quickly back into his chariot and rode off in a cloud of dust.

As his horses approached the palace walls, one of his servants ran out to greet him. 'You must get away! You must get away!' the man gasped, breathlessly.

'What do you mean?' asked Moses nervously.

'Pharaoh has just signed your death warrant!' said the servant. 'He has heard that you killed one of the slave drivers. He thinks you are about to lead an Israelite rebellion against him. You must leave—while you've got the chance!'

Moses gazed vacantly at the servant. Then he lashed his horses, turned the chariot round and drove away from the palace . . . away from his position . . . and away from his future. No longer was he a respected prince in Pharaoh's court, or an army commander. No longer was he God's deliverer of the Hebrew people. He was a murderer on the run. He was an enemy of both his adopted countrymen and his native ones. He had to get away! The only safe place was the wilderness. And yet, as he rode away from the palace for the last time, Moses somehow sensed that he was in God's will. He was not afraid any more.

Learning from Moses' mistakes

Like most of us, Moses knew what God wanted him to do—but rushed at it and took matters into his own hands. He lacked the maturity to realise that he simply wasn't ready for the tasks that lay ahead. He hadn't learned the critical lesson that when God raises up someone to do a job, he chooses them more on the basis of their character and their relationship with him than he does on their gifting, anointing and ability.

Of course, Moses' actions first in wanting to go back to his countrymen and then leaping to the aid of a defence-less slave were both commendable. But they were still wrong. If we look carefully at the circumstances, we can see why.

1. God-centred—or need-centred?

Moses' action was need-centred. He saw a slave needing help and acted in the heat of the moment. To him, the need represented the call to action. But he had to learn, as we do, that a leader who acts purely on the basis of people's needs won't last long. Sooner or later he will become overwhelmed with the enormity of the job in hand and will take on every burden that comes his way. He ends up becoming the saviour of his people—a role that only Jesus can fulfil. And when he finally and inevitably falls, his people become disillusioned and hurt. Moses had to learn to surrender to God his desires to help people and only take on the tasks he was given. Sadly, it would prove to be a lesson that he never fully grasped . . . for he made the same mistake again decades later. When faced with a human need—in this case, people's thirst—he would hit the rock with his staff rather than do what God had said and speak to it. The consequences were tragic: he missed out on the opportunity to lead his people into the Promised Land. A harsh lesson indeed, but one which illustrates that acting independently of God usually ends in trouble.

When Jesus saw people's needs, he was filled with compassion (Mt 9:36). Yet he only did the things he saw his Father doing. That's why he walked into the pool at Bethesda, healed one person and walked out again, leaving dozens of other sick people behind him.

That's why he almost certainly walked past the crippled man at the Gate Beautiful of the Jerusalem temple many times without saying 'Get up and walk' to him as he did to many other people in the same predicament. That's why he refused to respond to an urgent plea to go and heal his sick friend Lazarus until the time was right, even though he responded immediately to a similar request to help a centurion's daughter. Being God-centred rather than need-centred is difficult—and can appear at times to be unloving, and is guaranteed to make us unpopular at times. Yet it's the only way we will last the course in being a successful leader of God's people.

2. Waiting for God's timing

Moses' timing was wrong. He acted too soon. God's time to deliver the Israelites was still forty years away. The iniquity of the Amorites had not reached its full measure (Gen 15:16) and Moses' own education wasn't complete, either. He wasn't ready for the challenges that faced him—and neither were the Israelites, who had still to get to the point where they were genuinely prepared to forsake the false gods of Egypt and cry out for help to the God of their fathers from the bottom of their hearts—the basis for any successful and permanent deliverance.

An act performed for God at the right time is far more effective than a hundred carried out too soon—even if they are carried out with the right motives.

3. Trusting in God's strength

Moses acted in human strength—not under the anointing of God. Now Moses had every reason to be supremely confident in his ability to deliver his people—he had all the necessary training and qualifications. But as most of us need to find out sooner or later, training and qualifications don't necessarily mean much in the kingdom of God. You can train somebody into the ground, but unless they're anointed by God and are acting in obedience to him, they'll eventually fail. And conversely, you often find that the people who are the most successful leaders are the ones who don't have a qualification to their name—other than the all-important hand of God on their lives. Moses had to learn, as we do, that God uses the foolish things to confound the wise. Human might and power don't come into the equation when God is operating by his Spirit.

Moses put his hand up to his eyes to protect himself from the wind which was blasting clouds of sand into his face from across the desolate sand dunes. Wearily he stumbled towards a pile of rocks and sat down in an attempt to find some shelter. He was parched—his tongue was stuck to the roof of his mouth and his body was gradually dehydrating in the relentless heat. Pangs of hunger nagged inside him. He looked down at his sore and bleeding feet and shook his head—his fine leather shoes, a remnant of his days as a prince, had long since fallen to pieces. And if only he hadn't killed his horse! But there again, he hadn't had any choice—the animal was dying and he needed the meat to avoid starvation. Time and time again he cried out to his God—a silent, rasping cry, a cry of desperation. Yet there didn't seem to be an answer. Surely God hadn't preserved his life at birth, just to leave him to die a painful, anonymous death in the desert forty years later? After a while his strength gradually returned and he looked up. Was that an oasis in the distance? Perhaps. There were several of them in the wastes of Midian. Or maybe it was another mirage to mock him in his pain. With the help of his rod, Moses rose unsteadily to his feet and carried on walking, sweat pouring down his forehead and onto his dirty, matted beard, each step searing agony under the merciless desert sun. This wilderness was a terrible place, thought Moses. Created by God . . . but still a desperately terrible place.

Wilderness experiences

Sooner or later, if we mean business with God, he leads us into the wilderness. This is not a popular concept in some churches these days where there is an emphasis on a glorious and victorious problem-free existence, where everything is instamatic-automatic. But it's the only place where God can build a relationship with us of any real quality. It's easy to be 'going on with God' when things are working out well. But we discover the depth and extent of that relationship and what's really in our own hearts and in our lives when we're thrust into the wilderness. As the late Jamie Buckingham said in his excellent book *A Way Through the Wilderness*: 'The wilderness remains a place of purification and preparation—a place where a man can learn to distinguish between the clamouring voices of this world and the often quiet, gentle voice of God.'

And so God organises our circumstances like he did Moses'. One day we're fine—we're full of confidence, full of prophecy and ready to take on the world and the devil . . . and then suddenly, or maybe gradually, we find ourselves with our plans, our dreams and our visions lying in a heap at our feet, together with a load of Bible promises and faith-filled prayers. We feel confused, disappointed, disillusioned and betrayed—especially by God himself. It's a process that we must all face sooner or later. It happens to anybody who wants to be truly used by God to their full potential and to go beyond a fair-weather friendship with him. We come to a place where we hear God ask us what my friend Cathy Gibbs recently wrote in a very moving song . . . 'Will you still love me, even though your heart is breaking, even when my word does not come to pass?'

It happened to the apostle Paul. Yes, he had a Damascus Road experience which makes most of our supernatural encounters with God seem quite bland and insignificant. But while most of us in Paul's situation would have written a book about the incident and quickly become a main speaker at conferences and conventions, Paul still needed fourteen years on the sidelines, including around three years in the bleak Arabian desert before God could trust him with the history-shaping work of taking his gospel to the Gentiles.

It happened to Elijah. He spent years learning how to trust God during drought, famine and many other kinds of testing problems before he was ready for the spectacular firework display on Mount Carmel. And even afterwards, it was back to the wilderness again for this great prophet who then needed to understand that he wasn't the only person on earth whom God could use to bring about his purposes. Like all of us, he needed to discover that God is the only person who is indispensable.

It even happened to Jesus. None of us will ever understand what he went through in the rocky wilderness as he came face to face with Satan himself, was tested in his obedience to Scripture, and was tempted in all the ways we are in order to show us that the testing of our faith develops perseverance. As a result he returned with an anointing as well as an appointing. With all the emphasis on the anointing these days, it's easy to miss the important point—that it normally only comes through the suffering and testing that takes place in the wilderness.

And as we've seen, it happened to Moses, the forty-year-old prince who apparently had all the qualities needed to be a deliverer of God's people ... and yet who lacked the essential character qualities needed to be any real use to God or his people. A spell in the wilderness—and in his case it was a very long one—was the only way that God could refine him so that he could be trusted with the daunting task of leading his people into freedom and forming them into a nation.

How wilderness experiences happen

Spells in the wilderness are never organised by us. They would be no use whatsoever if we had any control over them. The whole point of them is that they test us to see what we are like and how we react when things happen that are out of our control. After all, the Christian life is more about reactions than actions. The wilderness is all about sorting out our 'flesh', and that 'flesh' will resist a wilderness experience if it possibly can and will generally plot and scheme a quick way out once we're in it! If we were to decide 'I think I need a spell in the wilderness,' that would devalue the experience, since it would be we, and not God, who were in the driving seat. The wilderness is the place where God tries to get us out of the driving seat so that he can get in and begin to work out his purposes in our lives without too much interference from us!

So how do wilderness experiences occur? Although only God himself knows the full answer to this question, there are three general principles which enable us to trace his hand in our circumstances.

1. They are initiated by God himself

Jesus' spell in the wilderness happened directly after his baptism—not an uncommon time for Christians to face all kinds of trials and temptations as we are tested to see if we really meant what we said while receiving a ducking! And it was the Holy Spirit who orchestrated Jesus' forty-day spell there. While Luke and Matthew tell us that the Spirit led him into the wilderness, Mark says that Jesus was driven there by the Holy Spirit. The Greek word used here is *ekballo*—the same word used to describe the way Jesus drove the money changers out of the temple in Jerusalem... not a pleasant 'would you be so kind' invitation, but an instruction to leave that verged on the violent. The use of this word indicates to me that Jesus wasn't exactly enthusiastic about the prospect of a hungry holiday in the desert with just the devil and some wild animals for company. For if he had been, he would not have learned so much about himself, his Father or his enemy while he was there. Certainly, the initiative to go there did not come from Jesus himself. It wasn't on his agenda ... 'Today—get baptised ... tomorrow—spend forty days in the wilderness being tempted by Satan'! But it was on his Father's. He had to be driven there, for God needed to test his Son's obedience and his preparedness to face the unpleasant experiences of life. For if Jesus hadn't been able to cope with the pressures and trials of the wilderness, he may never have been able to say 'Not my will but yours be done,' in the Garden of Gethsemane three years later. Jesus needed a time in the wilderness to prepare him for the things that lay ahead, just the same as we all do. Hebrews 12 tells us that God disciplines all of his children because he loves them.

It's easy to blame the devil when the rug is suddenly pulled out from under our feet. But very often it's God who is doing the pulling! To quote John Barr: 'God is a bigger trouble-maker in your life than the devil.' He often stirs up problems for us and in doing so drives us into the wilderness for a while simply because we would never go there of our own accord. So when things in our lives suddenly go wrong, when prayers stop being answered, when prophecies don't get fulfilled and our friends begin to misunderstand us, this is the time to avoid grumbling, avoid fighting and to get alone with God to see what it is he's trying to teach us. We can be encouraged by Jesus—after he'd been tested in the wilderness he was able to return to Galilee in the power of the Spirit which had rested on him at his baptism. He went on to see some spectacular results in his ministry. Supernatural power which has not had a supernatural testing is rarely to be trusted.

2. They are produced by sin

Thankfully, Jesus' death on the cross means that we don't have to feel guilty about anything any more. His shed blood means we are completely delivered from the penalty that we deserve for our actions. I don't know about you, but I find it a massive relief to think that every time the devil accuses me of something that I've done wrong, God looks at the blood of Jesus and says: 'Not guilty—case dismissed.'

Unfortunately, however, God does not always deliver us from the *consequences* of our actions. If you rob a bank tonight (I trust you won't!) forgiveness is guaranteed, provided that you show genuine repentance and don't do it again. However, God will not spare you a few years of eating porridge. And if you sleep around before you are married, you can be forgiven—but you will probably have to live with the consequences of broken relationships, sexually transmitted diseases or unwanted children in the future. Our actions are like seeds—and we reap what we sow.

It's these *consequences* of our sin that create a wilderness in our lives. That's what happened to Moses. He followed the age-old pattern of sinning and then hiding which was started by Adam and Eve in the Garden of Eden. He murdered someone and then ran and hid.

If it's sin that has driven us into the wilderness it will only be repentance that will help to bring us out. We're not told how God dealt with the issue of murder in Moses' life but the shedding of another man's blood has never been something that God has treated lightly—he has been in favour of capital punishment right from the time of the first murder! Yet it shows us plenty about God's mercy and his heart to redeem us that he was prepared to trust the Ten Commandments to someone who had broken them in the past.

I've spent time in the wilderness as a result of undealt-with sin and it's not a pleasant place to be! The problem is that God allows us to stay there for as long as we like. If we decide to co-operate with him and to allow both him and other people to bring tender restoration and repentance to our lives, the dry spell can be relatively short, although not normally as short as we'd like! But if we wrestle with God and are determined to get our own way, then God usually allows us to sweat it out—even if it takes forty years to get us to a place of usefulness, as with Moses. It is sometimes frightening when God asks us to deal with the darker sides of our lives. The cost of obeying him can be very high and we can at first sight stand to lose more than we are likely to gain. But many have found that the cost of disobeying him can be even higher.

3. They are caused by other people or unforeseen circumstances

Norman Barnes once caused a stir at a big Christian event when he stated, very forcefully, during a talk that 'life isn't fair'. Some people were upset by the concept, because many of us hold onto the notion that because we are Christians we are somehow entitled to a candy-floss existence where we say 'Jesus is Lord' at a meeting and then live happily ever after. I wish it could be like that! If we're honest, we have to admit that both life and other people can often deal us some very hard and unfair blows . . . hard enough to cause us an unwelcome spell in the wilderness.

Perhaps your marriage has failed or you've been made redundant. Maybe you've been wrongly accused of something, badly treated by your parents or have been handled unjustly by your church leaders . . . the list of possibilities is endless. Whatever the situation, the chances are that life has been unfair—and it wasn't your fault. As a result we retreat into solitude. We back off in relationships, wear an invisible and yet very noticeable 'Keep off' sign round our necks and stop talking to God. In other words, we sulk!

Now such actions are quite understandable—but not especially helpful. At the end of the day it may be true that we have been treated unfairly and that we weren't responsible for other people's unkind actions towards us. But we are responsible for the way we respond to situations. I for one have found through bitter experience that sitting around and moping for too long simply makes the situation worse. It's only as we start to see God's hand in our lives that we realise things may not be as bad as we first thought.

At times like this it is essential to remember a key verse in Psalm 16: 'The boundary lines have fallen for me in pleasant places.' In other words, whatever bitter circumstances we are facing in life, we can be confident that none of them has caught God by surprise and that he has sovereignly allowed them to make his word become real

in our lives and to sort out our characters. He has ultimately set the boundaries in our lives and therefore wants
us to see our circumstances as pleasant—even when they
don't appear that way. That's not to minimise our pain or
ignore the difficulties that we often have to face. But
within it all, we've got God's written guarantee that 'all
things work together for good for those who love God'
(Rom 8:28). And there is little point in saying to God that
life isn't fair and that we haven't got what we deserve—
for if any of us really got what we deserve, we'd have
been rejected by God many years ago.

Wilderness experiences caused either by other people or
unforeseen circumstances can either make us bitter . . . or
they can make us better. The choice is down to us. And the
only difference between those two words is the letter 'I'.
Maybe it's the I in our lives that needs sorting out . . . and
as Moses found, the wilderness is a very good place for
God to do it! As Norman Barnes added in that controversial talk: 'Life may not be fair—but God is just.'

God's restoration programme

As we've already seen, Scripture is full of people who
went through times of desperate disillusionment. But we
also find that God's healing programme for them is often
the same. He starts by sending someone into their isolated
and miserable world to bring some company. These people don't normally wait for an invitation: if they did that,
they would wait for ever, for people in the wilderness
aren't normally very good company—they are too
wrapped up in their own solitude. They simply go, gently
and unobtrusively, because God tells them to.

Consider Elijah. After his triumph against the prophets
of Baal he ran away and simply wanted to die—not an

uncommon kick-back from spiritual warfare. He was alone—and seriously depressed. And yet God made sure that an angel was there to quietly comfort him . . . and to bring him some food. No great words from the Lord. No plans for the future or more visions of chariots and horsemen. Just a bit of company and something to eat.

Consider Paul. A man with blood on his hands, reeling from a face-to-face confrontation with the living God on the Damascus Road. He was blind and so shocked he couldn't eat or drink. And yet into his wilderness came a man called Ananias, who risked life and limb and went uninvited to help restore Saul through the laying on of hands—simply because God said 'Go.'

God will always have his angel, his Ananias, ready to help the person in the wilderness. For Moses, a murderer on the run in a strange country, came a Bedouin shepherd named Jethro.

So, several hundred miles apart, there was a headstrong forty-year-old Egyptian prince who had everything, and yet nothing that really mattered . . . and a wise old Midianite shepherd-priest who had nothing, and yet with the thing that really mattered—a relationship with God.

Maybe the Midianite was the only person on earth with the God-given qualities to help Moses reach his true potential.

5

A Man Being Restored

She was seventeen, slim, and very beautiful. Her dusky, mischievous good looks were clear to see, even though her body was completely covered by a long, black dress, even concealing her tiny bare feet. Her bright eyes flashed beneath her colourful veil which, in typical Bedouin tradition, was spangled with ornate jewels and other tiny trinkets.

Jethro broke off from an animated discussion with one of his brothers, looked up at his oldest daughter, and smiled with pride. His wife's choice of name for her had been so appropriate: Zipporah . . . little bird. She was carefree and full of gaiety, although, he reflected wryly, perhaps little birds weren't quite as headstrong and prone to outbursts of temper!

He put down his drink and called over to her. 'It's time to take the sheep down to the well to be watered. Tell your sisters to go with you to help you.'

Zipporah put aside some weaving that she was doing and prepared herself for the trek to the well.

Jethro watched in amusement as Zipporah attempted to round up her six younger sisters. Perhaps it would be

easier trying to round up the sheep—at least they didn't
have such strong wills of their own. But after a while the
girls, all aged between eight and sixteen, wandered off
towards the well, laughing and chatting noisily as they
swung their goatskin water carriers by the handles.

'Watch out for shepherds from other tribes! Remember,
we're strangers in this region,' Jethro called out to them as
they went on their way in the late afternoon heat.

Like any parent, Jethro was worried—and not without
good reason. He and his clan were camping in unfamiliar
territory. They had left the relative safety of the land of
Midian and had headed west into the Sinai peninsula,
driven there by the drought and the continual search for
water. The watering holes and wells of Midian had all dried
up in the summer sun, but they had heard that there were
still some supplies left in the Wilderness of Paran. Jethro
had initially been uneasy about taking his clan into alien
territory, but he had not had any choice—it was either that
or face the ravages of the drought and the inevitable
starvation which would result. After several weeks trekking through the sunbaked desolation of sand and volcanic
dust they had eventually discovered a tiny oasis with two
wells and a few clusters of date palms, surrounded by
hundreds of thirsty sheep and goats. Jethro's clan had
pitched their tents a few miles away and even though
they had been untroubled so far, they were still alert to
the threat from other clans and tribes. And as Jethro
watched his seven daughters disappear behind the craggy
rocks, he prayed that God would protect them from harm.

A while later, the girls arrived at the well with their
flocks. Zipporah looked around for possible danger but,
to her relief, everything seemed quiet. The place was
empty apart from a haggard-looking traveller who was
apparently resting under the shade of a nearby date palm.

Zipporah and her sisters knelt down at the well and started to draw the water in the way that people had done there for hundreds of years. It was hot, tedious work—they needed to fill as many carriers full of water as they could in order to give the flocks a sufficient evening feed. The sheep only fed in the evening during most of the year, spending the rest of the day trying to find precious places of shade among the trees, rocks and bushes.

Suddenly there were angry, raucous shouts from the other side of the oasis. 'Get away! This well is ours!' Zipporah looked up to see where the shouts had come from and saw several shepherds running towards her, waving their clubs. She and her sisters had been so busy drawing the water that they hadn't noticed the men arrive with flocks of their own. She jumped up in fear and shouted to her sisters. Some of the younger girls screamed in terror and dropped their water carriers as the shepherds drew closer, shouting obscenities at them and making violent gestures with their clubs. 'Get away, Midianites,' they growled. 'Get back to your own land before we kill you.'

No one had taken much notice of the traveller sitting under the date palm. But he had been watching the scene closely and now suddenly leapt to his feet and darted towards the shepherds, his fists swinging. As Moses rounded on the astonished shepherds, he felt the desire to kill coursing through his veins again. He caught the nearest man with a blow across the back, knocking him to the ground. The other shepherds stopped harassing Zipporah and her sisters and looked at him in astonishment. Although they were tough men of the desert and were well used to fighting, they quickly realised that this was not a man to trifle with. He was tall and powerfully built and carried a worrying sense of confidence about him. The expression on his face made it clear that he was not making idle threats. They looked at one another fleetingly and then ran off into the safety of some nearby rocks. Moses stood there for several minutes, still poised and ready to lash out until he was certain that the danger had passed.

He looked tough and confident, but in fact his mind was starting to race in confusion. Grimly he realised that he was afraid. It was not the shepherds . . . they were no threat to a trained soldier like himself. No, he was afraid of himself, or of the person he was becoming. It was bad enough committing murder once. But now it had almost happened again. He knew that he had not been in control of himself when he had hit that shepherd. Had the man resisted, he would surely have battered him to death, without hesitation or mercy. Dark forces wrestled inside Moses. And he knew he needed help.

Slowly he relaxed and regained his composure. Then he looked around for the girls. They were nowhere to be seen. He called to them to come out. Silence. He called out again. And then a tall, veiled Bedouin girl emerged tentatively from behind a rock fifty yards away. Moses waved to her. The girl stood up and as she did so, six others nervously followed.

Moses walked towards them, his eyes twinkling with amusement at the sight of the seven Bedouin girls, each one slightly taller than the next, the older ones veiled, the younger ones with their faces still uncovered. 'Don't be afraid,' he said as the girls drew closer to him. His eyes lingered briefly on the oldest girl. She was someone of breathtaking beauty—even more stunning than the girls in the Egyptian palaces. Their luxurious clothes and fine perfumes and oils were outdone by this young shepherd girl's innocent simplicity. She met his gaze and then lowered hers with embarrassment.

'Let me feed your flocks for you. That will be safer,' Moses said to her.

Two hours later, as the sun started to disappear behind the hill tops, Moses finished watering the sheep and the girls began rounding them up ready for the trek back to the camp. Normally Zipporah and her sisters would have remained at the well for longer, but this time she decided they should return to their camp straight away in case there was any further danger from the shepherds. And she still did not feel completely comfortable with this stranger. Although she knew that he was kind and felt attracted to him, there was something intimidating behind his friendly exterior . . . something that she couldn't put her finger on. What was he doing there?

Zipporah smiled shyly at Moses from behind her veil, thanked him for his help, and began organising her sisters ready for the walk back to the tents.

As the girls walked off into the dusty distance with their flocks, Moses went and sat down once more under the date palm, alone again. Alone with his thoughts, alone with his guilt, and with images of murder and bloodshed still torturing his mind.

Zipporah and her sisters ran breathlessly up to their father's tent. Jethro looked up at her inquiringly. 'Why have you returned so early today?' he asked.

'An Egyptian rescued us from some shepherds!' they gasped, excitedly. 'He even drew water for us and watered the flock.'

'And where is he?' Jethro asked his daughters. 'Why did you leave him? Invite him to have something to eat!' Jethro was annoyed that the girls had not offered the stranger the traditional Bedouin hospitality, especially since he had evidently done so much to help them.

'Shall I go and fetch him?' asked Zipporah, both excited and a little frightened at the prospect of seeing the man again.

'Yes, go and invite him to join us for a meal,' said Jethro. 'Tell him he can stay with us. And get your mother and sisters to bake fresh bread and slaughter a goat for a special feast.'

Zipporah's heart was beating as she returned to the well. So was Jethro's . . . even though he could not understand why.

There is an old Bedouin legend attached to Zipporah's walk back to the camp with the fugitive Moses. The story goes that after Zipporah had found Moses again at the well, she walked ahead of him to show him the way. But the crisp evening wind began to blow and lifted her dress slightly to reveal her legs—a display almost akin to nakedness in the Bedouin culture. So Moses, we are told, saved her further embarrassment by calling to her, saying: 'It would be better if you walked behind me and told me when to turn left or right.' And since then, all Bedouin women have walked behind their men. Whether or not this legend is true, what we do know is that as the sun set across the vast wastes of the Sinai peninsula, Moses and Jethro met one another . . . and, like many things in God's kingdom, an unexpected encounter turned out to be one that would alter the course of human history.

Jethro put down his rough stone bowl and looked at Moses thoughtfully. They had enjoyed a fine meal together—freshly slaughtered goat laced with herbs and made into a delicious stew, served by the women with bread, freshly baked over the crackling fire. Now they were relaxing, sipping date wine and chatting under the same stars where God had spoken to Abraham all those years before. The conversation had been friendly and warm but, in keeping with the strict rules of Bedouin hospitality, was quite superficial and a little formal. They had spoken about the desert, about the sheep and about the weather. Strangers were never asked 'Where are you from?' or 'What do you want?' To ask such a question was thought to be the height of rudeness, even in circumstances when an explanation might have been considered appropriate. A Bedouin would perhaps never discover a stranger's real reason for passing through. Offering hospitality unconditionally was seen as far more important than finding out somebody's business. Perhaps we could take a leaf out of the Bedouins' book of hospitality today.

But Jethro was none the less puzzled. Who was this man, this strong, powerfully built Egyptian who had told Zipporah that he was a Prince? What was he doing here in the desert, far beyond the regions that Egyptian raiding parties normally went? Why was he wearing expensive but tattered clothes? And his eyes . . . why did they have a look of haunted desperation about them? Jethro put the questions out of his mind, poured out more wine and continued chatting.

Maybe the truth would come out later.

Moses sat in the cool of the evening, watching as Zipporah sat outside one of the tents, grinding some grain between a big millstone some eighteen inches across. She carefully poured some grain through a whole in the middle and then grasped a handle on the upper stone and revolved it so that the grain was crushed in the middle. The revolution of the stones made a rough, rasping sound—a sign of life and prosperity among Bedouin communities. If the noise of flour grinding stopped, the silence spelled poverty and desolation and bleak times for the family.

Moses looked away and thought for a while before speaking to Jethro, who was sitting on a rough goatskin mat on the other side of the tent. Moses had something on his mind. Eventually, he plucked up courage and spoke.

'Which god do you serve?' he asked Jethro tentatively. 'Is he the same as the ones I have heard of in Egypt—the sun god Re or the river god Osiris?'

'No, neither of those,' replied Jethro. 'My clan and I all worship the invisible God of our father Abraham. He has no name and no image. But we called him God Elohe as our forefather Jacob did. We believe that he is the only true God. The gods you refer to are all to do with the forces of nature. Most gods are. But God is the one who created nature, who created the world itself, right at the beginning of time.'

Moses' heart missed a beat. God! The God of his ancestors! 'I've heard of this God,' he exclaimed in surprise. 'My parents told me about him,' he continued. 'You see, I am one of his people! I am not really an Egyptian. I am an Israelite.'

So that was it! Jethro had been curious about Moses' nationality ever since he'd first met him. Although he had introduced himself as an Egyptian, the story hadn't rung true—his features did not resemble those of the Egyptians whom Jethro had occasionally seen in the desert regions around Dophkah. Obviously there was more to this man than met the eye, but he decided not to ask too many questions in case he caused offence. Instead he told him about his forefather Midian, who was one of Abraham's sons, and how his tribe, the Midianites, was formed.

Moses sat and listened in fascination as Jethro unwittingly continued to fill in details of his ancestral background over the generations—about how God spoke to Abram in the desert regions and promised him that he would become the father of many nations when he was almost one hundred and his wife, Sarai was ninety—way beyond child bearing years . . . and how God was faithful and gave Sarai a son named Isaac. Moses had heard some of it before through things he had picked up and people he had met in the royal palace. But there was plenty that he had never heard about before.

Jethro went on to describe how Isaac produced two sons, Jacob and Esau, and how Jacob in turn had twelve sons who became leaders of the twelve tribes of Israel. Then he told him about Joseph and how his brothers had sold him into slavery, only for Jethro's tribe, the Midianites, to buy him and sell him to the Egyptians. 'God's hand was on his life and he eventually became the man in charge of all Egypt, second only to the King himself,' Jethro continued. Moses' ears pricked up at the reference to Egypt. The story was starting to make some sense now. Jethro poked the fire with a stick, stirring the embers into life, and resumed the tale.

'Joseph's family were eventually reunited and went to live in Egypt,' he said. 'They lived there until he was one hundred and ten. Apparently he lived to see three generations of children before God finally took him. The story goes that he was embalmed and placed in a coffin in Egypt, in the hope that his bones would one day be returned to his homeland. Maybe you've seen his tomb?' Moses shook his head. 'Anyway, a new king eventually came to power in Egypt. He had never heard of Joseph or his people. He saw the Israelites as a threat and forced them into slavery. And that's the way it's been for them for several hundred years now. From what I hear from travelling merchants, they are still leading a miserable life and are being savagely treated by their task masters.'

Moses shuddered inwardly as the story started to cut close to home. Memories of the murdered Egyptian slave driver came flooding back. He went pale. Jethro noticed the slight change in the atmosphere, but continued. 'So tell me,' he went on, deciding that now was the time to press home a direct question. 'How did you come to be in the courts of the King of Egypt?'

'It's a long story,' said Moses. 'You mentioned the new king in Egypt who forced the Israelites into slavery. Well, he also issued a decree that all Hebrew boys should be thrown into the River Nile as soon as they were born. As you say, he saw the Israelites as a threat and wanted to destroy them. Now when I was born, my mother hid me for three months in her home instead of allowing me to be killed. But when I was too big to hide any more, she got a papyrus basket and coated it with pitch and tar and put me in it. Then she left it on the banks of the Nile to see what would happen to me. Later on the king's daughter came down to the river to bathe, saw the basket and sent one of her slave girls to go and fetch it. She opened it and saw me inside, crying.' Moses paused for a moment and chuckled with embarrassment. 'She realised that I was one of the Hebrew babies and felt sorry for me. My sister Miriam was there and asked the king's daughter if she wanted a Hebrew woman to come and nurse the baby. She agreed, and Miriam went and got my mother.

'My mother took me away and nursed me until I was older and then one day she took me back to Pharaoh's daughter and I became her son. I can just about remember her taking me there. So I became a prince and grew up in the king's palaces. It was a grand life and I learned the wisdom of the Egyptians. I even became a soldier in their army.' Moses was silent for a while and his eyes suddenly filled with tears. 'But I still wish I could meet my real mother and father—that would be wonderful. They must have loved me very much to save my life in the way that they did.' His voice faltered. 'I wonder what they would think of me now. . . .'

Jethro sat listening intently, but said nothing. He sensed that Moses wanted to say more. There was a period of quietness as Moses stared at the floor, his face wracked with pain and confusion.

It was Jethro who broke the silence. For some reason, he felt he should speak more about God. As he started speaking, it was as if the words were not his own . . . 'From what my forefathers tell me, right at the beginning of time, God created the heavens and the earth and he made man and woman and set them in a beautiful garden. Legend has it that it was not far away from here. The man was called Adam and the woman was called Eve and they lived lives of close friendship with God. He told them they could enjoy the garden and eat its fruit, but they should not eat fruit from the tree of knowledge of good and evil. But they disobeyed him and ate from it and because they did wrong, God banished them from the garden for ever. Yet even though Adam disobeyed God and was punished for it, God still showed kindness to him and to Eve. He killed animals and used their skins to make clothes to cover them. And some people say it wasn't just their nakedness that was covered. The blood of the animals also covered their wrong doing, so that God did not hold it against them any more. God's heart is always to forgive the things we have done wrong and to restore us whenever he can.'

Tears began flowing down Moses' face and Jethro moved across the tent and embraced him, just as he often embraced his own son, Hobab. After a while Moses managed to gasp out the words, 'Do you think . . . do you think that God can ever forgive an act of . . . murder?' And as the night grew darker, Moses spoke . . . about himself, about his shattered dreams of delivering God's people . . . and about the awful murder that was torturing his conscience. And throughout it all, Jethro listened. It was the night that was the starting point of change in Moses' life.

A listening ear

Moses probably discovered, as we all do eventually, that what he needed was a listener . . . someone who doesn't say much, but who is simply there, not to criticise, not to counsel, not to rebuke, but just to listen. Sadly, listeners are rare in our busy churches these days. Everybody wants to be a mouth in the body of Christ—but few of us want to be an ear! As a result, people with a 'need' are simply given a counselling appointment in the pastor's busy diary—and after their half-hour session, that's it. They normally go away frustrated. But many people need more time than that—and counselling is very often the last thing they need! That's the problem you can get when there is one busy pastor trying to look after a church full of people.

I remember once I was going through a very rough time and fearing I might drift away from God and his people altogether. There was sin in my life—and I didn't really care any more. One night my housegroup leader arrived at my house and announced that we were going out for a curry. I was suspicious—he obviously had an agenda and basically I didn't really want to know. But he was friendly enough and I've never been known to refuse a tandoori. So I went.

That night he helped God to restore my life. How? Simply by listening to me—for several hours. He hardly said a word. No clever answers or amazing words of knowledge. No prophecies and advice on how to get my life straightened out. Just a listening ear, a kind heart and eyes that didn't glaze over with boredom after ten minutes. But by the following day I knew that God had done a work in my heart—simply because someone had bothered to listen. Healing and repentance followed quickly.

That incident reminded me of something that the well-known Spring Harvest speaker Alex Buchanan once said while speaking publicly. He recollected how he'd spent years going from Christian to Christian, just trying to find someone to listen to him—someone to whom he could pour out his heart. It took him a long time to discover that person.

Listening is costly. It is also boring at times. Counselling can be relatively easy. If you counsel someone you set
a time limit on how long you're prepared to spend with
them, just like a doctor or a dentist, and when they've used
up their time, off they go. And if we're honest, most of the
session isn't spent listening to the person—it's spent
waiting for them to stop talking so that we can jump in
with a wise word or amazing revelation and get on with
the next engagement in the diary. And while this approach
may help some people, it's unlikely to succeed with
people who are in the pits of despair or who are struggling with serious issues in their lives . . . perhaps even
their faith itself. We must be prepared to draw alongside
them, probably uninvited, and give them time. Lots of
time. Time with no strings attached. In other words, we
should simply offer friendship, like Jethro did to Moses—
not because we're expecting a certain result or are waiting
for the magic moment when we can sort them out, but
because we care enough to actually like them.

Questions are important, though, providing we know
what to ask and how to ask it. The Holy Spirit will help
us, if we ask him to. A few years ago I spent time with a
young woman who was seriously depressed and was
suffering from anorexia and other mental and emotional
problems. After a while, I felt completely out of my depth.
She was so negative and gloomy that there didn't seem to
be a way to help her. So I just kept on sending mental SOS
prayers to God and asking her questions . . . nothing clever,
just ordinary everyday questions about her family and her
friends and how she was feeling about different situations.
Suddenly it was as if a light had been switched on inside her
head. Unbeknown to me, my 'random', almost desperate,
questions had been inspired by the Spirit and they gradually
formed a pattern which helped this lady see where her

problems really lay. She went away rejoicing that day, and I don't know who was more surprised—her or me!

Situations like this don't happen every day, but we can trust the Holy Spirit, who is sometimes described in Scripture as the finger of God, to put that finger right on the things that matter in someone's life. Asking questions will help to draw the person out . . . ones which can't be answered with a 'yes' or 'no'. But listening is the key. I believe it was the key that unlocked Moses' life—and unlocked a new man, capable of one day becoming a true leader of God's people. Not filled with ambition and with the wisdom of the Egyptians. But filled with love, meekness and the wisdom of God.

Dawn was approaching and the sky was still gunmetal grey. Jethro lay on his rough straw bed, unable to sleep. His mind was still racing with the events of the evening. The previous night had been bad enough, trying to come to terms with playing host to an Egyptian prince. But a murderer, on the run from the king of Egypt—that was a different proposition altogether. He rolled over, trying to work out what he was feeling about the whole situation. A large part of him liked Moses—he had warmed to him as soon as he had met him for the first time, just two days earlier. And he certainly had sympathy for his plight. But a murderer . . . that was different. Jethro had been brought up on the principle that shedding the blood of another was wrong and had to be avenged. He felt a strong sense of revulsion about offering hospitality to a man who had the blood of another man on his hands, and a strong sense of justice about the situation, too. Maybe he ought to tell Moses to leave. But no . . . that would breach the Bedouin code of hospitality. Moses was entitled to enjoy the safety and security of Jethro's family while he remained there with them.

But as the sun rose at the start of another blistering day, Jethro had decided what to do. He would ask Moses to leave. After all, he had given him the customary three and a third days among his family. What else could he do? Yes, he'd provide him with water and provisions for his journey and that would be the end of it. That way his hands would be clean. . . . And yet, and yet . . .

As Jethro turned the situation over and over in his mind, the voice of God spoke into his heart. 'Be a father to Moses.'

Jethro froze inside. Father . . . to a murderer! Jethro emerged from his tent into the bright morning sunlight and stroked his beard thoughtfully. And he realised, once again, that God was a God who always did the unexpected.

God's army of failures

Murderers. Liars. Adulterers. Deceivers. The pages of the Bible are full of them. And yet they are the people of God— and the people whom God used, and still uses, in the most remarkable ways to get his will done on earth. It has always been his heart to write on the write-offs—and it still is. And yet while we all give mental assent to the principle that God uses the foolish to confound the wise, we sometimes find it difficult to put the idea into practice. How many of us would put Simon Peter on a leadership training course, just days after he had renounced his relationship with Jesus completely—let alone trust him with the leadership of a new church, several thousand strong? How many of us would allow David to remain king after he had committed adultery and arranged someone's murder? And, to bring the illustrations up to date, how many of us would be prepared to give positions of trust and responsibility to,

say, a former IRA terrorist or a drag queen who had
undergone a sex change operation, if they'd genuinely
turned to God and brought their pasts to a conclusion?
It's a risky business, as Jesus found when he trusted the
money bag to Judas. But it's a risk we all have to be
prepared to take if we really want to see God work out
his purposes in a dynamic way. If we fail to do so we will
end up with middle-class churches which are led by the
'right' sort of people but which are incapable of reaching
out with compassion or understanding to the ordinary
people and the sinners. If God is prepared to take a risk
with someone, then so should we be . . . and of course we
will always have the reassurance that it is he who will take
bottom line responsibility if things go wrong.

'God has been good to me,' Jethro remarked to Moses as
they walked together through the sparse brown desert
pastures, surrounded by hundreds of sheep and goats.
'Just look at these flocks! Even though there have been
times when many have died due to the drought, God has
always remained faithful and has blessed me. Now . . .
well, there are too many of them to count. He has made
me a wealthy man, just the same as he did Abraham.'

The two of them walked a little further in silence. It was
now several days since Moses had first arrived among
Jethro's people and he was unsure whether or not he
was still welcome.

Jethro cleared his throat and stopped walking. 'Moses,'
he said. 'When you first arrived I greeted you with the
words *"Ahlan wa sahlan"* . . . "You are part of the
family." That's the greeting that we Bedouin people give
to any visitors who pass by. But to you, these words have a
special meaning. I would like you to become part of my

family, part of my clan—for good. I know that you have
been brought up as an Egyptian and that some of my
people will not like a foreigner joining them. You may
have to face prejudice and resentment at times. And I
know that you have killed a man and it will take a long
time before my people trust a man with blood on his
hands. But I believe that God himself is in all this and
that it is his will that you are here. I would like you to join
us . . . to be the same to me as my own son Hobab: a real
son. And maybe I can help you to become the man that
God originally intended you to be. You can certainly help
me—I would like you to learn the ways of a shepherd and
look after my flocks for me. What do you think?'

Moses listened in silence and then suddenly threw his
arms around the man who had already become like a
father to him during the few days that he had known
him . . . the father he had never known. 'Yes, I would
like to stay,' he said simply. 'Where else can I go?'

'It won't be easy,' warned Jethro. 'Life in the desert is
very tough—there are none of the fine wines and comfortable living that you are used to in the palaces of Egypt.
Out here, we are in a constant battle to find water and the
elements can be very cruel at times. Food is often short.
And the work of a shepherd is demanding. When you are
looking after sheep you have to feed them, defend them
and care for them, no matter what the cost. You have to be
prepared to die for them if necessary.' Moses nodded. 'But
who knows?' Jethro resumed. 'Perhaps if you can prove
yourself faithful looking after my sheep and goats and can
learn to live the simple life of desert people, then maybe
one day God will trust you sufficiently to let you be a
deliverer to his people after all . . .'

This time, Moses shook his head. No. That part of his
life was over.

6

A Man with a Mentor

The Jethro ministry

If we're serious about leadership, then one thing's for sure: we may never make it without a Jethro.

He, or she, will be the person who trains us, shapes us and who generally puts up with us while God is preparing us for his purposes. They will believe in us when nobody else does, understand us when everyone else thinks we've taken leave of our senses, and stand by us when everyone else has done a runner.

Their influence on our lives will be incalculable. Yet sadly, the Jethro ministry is sometimes a scarce commodity in our churches nowadays. It is often replaced with courses and books, and while these things are helpful in their own way, the personal input of a man or woman who has been through the mill already simply cannot be replaced.

We don't know an awful lot about Jethro. History is divided as to whether or not Jethro was a follower of God. The Bible perhaps indicates that he was. He first appears, unannounced, in Exodus 2, bearing the name of Reuel, which means Friend of God, a name which was presumably chosen by his parents to indicate his family's relationship with the Almighty. And he was quick to say, 'Praise be to the Lord,' when Moses told him about the Passover in Exodus 18:10. Significantly, Jethro then went on to fulfil his priestly function by sacrificing some animals—to God. However we do not know whether his relationship with God went as far as entering into the covenant of circumcision.

One legend has it that Jethro was so uncompromising about his relationship with God that he was ostracised by other Midianites and went off with his son and daughters to live alone. It's not clear whether or not this is true, but the facts certainly tend to suggest that Jethro was a true follower of God.

He was a Midianite, a tribe which can be traced back to Midian, who was the fourth son of Abraham's concubine Keturah. The story goes that one day Abraham gave Midian and Keturah's other sons gifts of goats, ewes, rams, cows, bulls and donkeys and sent them off into the south-eastern part of the Sinai peninsula to start lives of their own—church plants, 1800 BC style!

Midian and his sons had families of their own which grew to form several clans and over the years they became a tribe, populating the desert borders of the Transjordan from Moab down past Edom. They were not Jews and were never counted among God's chosen people. But their foundations ran deep and they certainly knew the God of their forefather Abraham for themselves and many of them followed him.

The Midianites became a proud, aggressive people who frequently lived up to their name, which meant strife or contention . . . they were famed for their violent clashes with other tribes. They populated the desert for hundreds of years, some of them working as shepherds and others working in the copper mines of the Arabah. They and the Ishmaelites were the people who bought the boy Joseph from his scheming brothers for twenty shekels of silver and later sold him into slavery.

Reuel eventually became a leader of the Midianites, undoubtedly earning the position by winning the respect of the other tough clansmen over the years. He would have been a brave, powerfully built man, daring and courageous as a shepherd. He was probably wealthy by Bedouin standards and as a priest he would have been deeply respected by his people. His duties would have involved settling inter-family disputes and arguments over land with the heads of other Midianite clans, and he would probably have been involved in performing animal sacrifices as a thanksgiving to God. He would have gathered his clans together on special occasions, slain a new-born lamb and then presided over a joyful thanksgiving meal which would have lasted late into the night with music, dancing and other festivities.

It's not clear when, or why, Reuel changed his name to Jethro—or whether it was a decision he took himself or one that went with his priestly appointment. But there is enormous significance in the names. As we have seen, Reuel means Friend of God; Jethro means Excellence, or Pre-eminence. I'm sure that Jethro was not the first person in Scripture who discovered that excellence in God's kingdom can only come from being a friend of God.

I am sometimes amazed at the people God raises up to perform various tasks. They are the last people I'd choose! But perhaps he chooses them because they've got the one qualification that matters: they are friends of God. People he can count on. People he can trust. People who've proved their loyalty and their faithfulness to him in good times and in bad, in big things and small. There's a list of them in Romans 16. Paul singles out unknowns like Apelles, Rufus and Epenetus for a special pat on the back. They were God's friends who had helped Paul out at different times. Scripture's unsung heroes.

A couple who are very close to me are friends of God. Their names are Keith and Lorraine. There they were, doing their studies at university, and then quite suddenly, God called them to be missionaries. Now they're serving him with Wycliff Bible Translators in Africa. Many people were surprised when they announced their plans all those years ago. I wasn't. For although they weren't that experienced and had not really 'done' much in church, they were God's friends. Not much else mattered. That's why they're succeeding now in their calling.

The Bible says that there were only two men who held the office of priest before Moses set up the formal priesthood, first through Aaron and his sons and then later through the Levites. The first recorded priest was Melchizedek. The second was Jethro.

They were, without doubt, men of some influence. The Hebrew word to describe their office is *kohen*, which means a chief ruler, or a principal office—a leader of some significance. That is why Melchizedek is also referred to as the Prince of Salem (probably Jerusalem) and Jethro is occasionally called the Prince of the Midianites. They were like royalty among their people. In fact you could say that they were among the rare Old Testament characters who took on the triple anointing that Jesus carried of prophet, priest and king.

Without Jethro, Moses would never have become the man who delivered Israel. For although the Scriptures only refer to him fleetingly, the impact this old shepherd had on Moses' life must have been incalculable. So what were the qualities that enabled Jethro to be the man who restored Moses?

1. He had a low profile

Scripture only refers to Jethro fleetingly. He could hardly be called a major Old Testament character—or at least, not by our way of looking at it! But maybe that's because our God is one who has always remained true to the principles in 1 Corinthians 12:22–24 which talk about giving greater honour to the people who are apparently weaker and insignificant in our eyes.

And yet Jethro leaves a permanent footprint in history—and an influence which goes well beyond the number of verses he occupies in Scripture. He humbled himself, playing second fiddle to a seemingly greater man like Moses—and let God exalt him. It's all about putting other people first—an easy thing to miss when there is considerable emphasis nowadays on developing *our* gift, *our* ministry and *our* anointing! You see plenty of courses where we are encouraged to develop ourselves—but not so many where we are taught to train others to the point where they overtake us! And yet this is the heart of a real ministry from God. Jesus demonstrated it in leaving his church to fulfil a greater task than he ever carried out himself.

2. He was a servant

Whenever you read about Jethro in Scripture, it is in the context of serving. We find him offering hospitality, offering refuge and offering advice in a quiet, unobtrusive way. He was not a leader who served. He was a *servant* who happened to lead. There's all the difference in the world between the two. The same applies today, especially in our churches where we have had around twenty years or more of emphasis on re-establishing and strengthening the role of a leader. Elders are *not* called to be leaders! They are called to serve through leading (Mt 20:25–28). Dale Rumble expresses this even more clearly in his excellent book *The Diakonate* (Torbay Publishing Ltd): 'Elders and deacons are a corporate diakonate for an assembly, since they jointly serve the flock. I have often heard it said "Deacons are to serve, but elders are to rule". We need to settle it in our hearts that all ministry functions, all those in leadership in the church, are servants.'

The most important thing an elder or a leader can do for their people is to set a good example by being a servant. That's what Jethro was. He didn't have to teach about servanthood. He *was* servanthood!

The apostle Peter makes the point well in his first letter (chapter 5:1–4): 'Be shepherds of God's flock that is under your care, *serving* as overseers—not because you must but because you are willing, as God wants you to be; not greedy for money, but *eager to serve*; not lording it over those entrusted to you, but *being examples to the flock.*'

3. He released a significant ministry

The hallmark of real men and women of God is that they release other people's ministries, not their own. You never see Jethro promoting himself—but you do see him bringing God into the life of Moses in remarkable ways, as we shall see in the chapters ahead. And yet despite Moses' fame and success later in life, Jethro's own role never changed, as far as we know. He remained behind the scenes until he died. But he certainly contributed to Moses' success. It's an awesome plumbline of our effectiveness for God—not how successful *we* are, but how successful *other people* are because of us!

4. He had no earthly ties

Occasionally you stumble across people in Scripture and wonder if they were really human or were some kind of angel! Enoch was one of them. All we know about him was that he walked with God for 750 years, and then 'God took him away'. The text may imply that he didn't even die.

Jethro is another. He simply emerges in the pages of Scripture and disappears again. There's no record of his birth, his family or his death.

There's something about people like Enoch, and possibly Jethro, that I find deeply challenging. It's almost as though they were so caught up with God, so engrossed in their relationship with him, that an earthly existence was almost incidental. Parents, birth and even death didn't seem to matter that much. Only God mattered. Nothing else.

I once knew a dear lady called Paula who had a relationship with God like that. She was totally consumed with God. She sadly died of a heart attack when she was thirty-seven, leaving a husband and three children—an enormous human tragedy. But someone at her funeral put it very well. 'We know she's in heaven now, because she was so close to God she was almost there already.' What a wonderful tribute to a woman of God—she loved him so much, and was more caught up with the things of heaven than the relative trivialities of the things of earth. This attitude helped her to be the enormously loving person that she was.

I wish I could say that my love for God, and my relative 'hatred' for the world, was like that!

5. He was hospitable

The first time Jethro met Moses, he offered him a meal. That's because he was a man with God's heart for hospitality. Jesus was the same. The first thing he did when he

met two of John's disciples was to invite them to spend
the day with him (Jn 1:35–39). Wherever you see God's
man or woman, you'll always find an open door to match
the open heart—and probably an open fridge or food
cupboard, too!

For Jethro, hospitality was part of his culture. He and
his people took enormous pleasure in welcoming strangers
into their tents. And they would share their food and water
with them—even if they only had a tiny piece of bread
left.

Strangers would be greeted with the words '*Ahlan wa
sahlan*' ('You are part of our family') and ushered out of
the heat and into the tents. Inside, they would be offered a
drink and something to eat. Particularly important guests
would receive a special honour—a goat would be slain
and cooked especially for them. For a Bedouin, this was a
great sacrifice, since for him his entire wealth lay in his
flock. And turning down a Bedouin's hospitality was the
equivalent to insulting him.

Strangers would never be asked who they were or what
they wanted. The welcome was automatic and they could
make themselves at home with the rest of the family for
just over three days. While they were there they were
entitled to share in the family's food, water, protection
and other privileges.

So to Jethro, being hospitable was not an effort—and
not even a matter of choice. It was part of everyday life—
as much an instinct as protecting his flocks.

We live in a western culture where intruders and strangers are resented and treated with suspicion. Even our
friends are brushed aside with an answering machine or
a quick chat on the doorstep. Perhaps we all need to look
again at people like Jethro and ask God to deal with the
fear which stops us being like them and from living in

genuine *koinonia* (community) like the New Testament church did. Because for many people who are hurt and lonely, '*Ahlan wa sahlan*' is all they need to hear.

6. He was a father figure

It's doubtful whether Moses ever knew his real father, Amram. The nearest thing he would have had to a father figure as he grew up was probably Pharaoh himself. That is, of course, until Jethro entered his life. And although Jethro became Moses' father-in-law, it wasn't long before he took on the role of Moses' adopted father, too. Significantly, Moses' ministry only started to develop usefully for God once he had a father figure in his life.

We all need a father figure in our lives . . . not just a real father, but a spiritual father, too. I remember counselling a man once who was finding it hard to get moving in his ministry in church life. 'God will never release you until you have a spiritual father,' I told him. He cried— and within months God had shown him a man who was ideal for the job. His ministry grew and flourished from that point. Why? Because he felt secure. He felt safe. He had someone there for him, to advise him, to encourage him, to give him the occasional wise rebuke and to give him a hug of reassurance when things were tough. You can't put a price on a ministry like that—and you often find that ministries without fathers are insecure and potentially dangerous.

Ultimately, God is our Father, if we believe in him. The Bible reveals him as a Father who created us (Mal 2:10), a collective Father to all his people (Mal 1:6), and a Father who adopts us as his children (Gal 3:26 and Jn 1:13). One of Jesus' main reasons for coming to live on the earth was to reveal himself as the Way . . . the way to his Father, a Father who is loving, tender, faithful and vigilant in his care for us. He wants us all to call him 'dad', just the same as he did.

But we need human spiritual fathers, too . . . people who can be 'God with skin on', as a little boy once described it when he was scared and wanted a hug from his dad during a storm one night. Although it's a wonderful privilege to pray to Our Father, it's just as wonderful and equally important to have a trusting relationship with a spiritual father, like Elisha did with Elijah and Timothy did with Paul.

It was the Father in heaven who released Moses into his ministry of leading the Jewish people. But it was Jethro, his father on earth, who got him ready for it—and made such an impression on him that Moses was able to fulfil the same role with Joshua later on.

Zipporah's heart was beating rapidly, just like any bride's on her wedding day. She smiled tentatively as her father, Jethro, her mother and a throng of Bedouin women escorted her to her tent amid claps and cheers from the rest of her clan.

One of the women drew back the curtain to the women's section of the tent and ushered her in, accompanied by the others. There were giggles and squeals of laughter over the next hour as the women—some of them Zipporah's sisters—helped her get ready for her bridegroom. Then in typical Bedouin tradition they left, one by one, until just one—an older woman, called the nurse for the sake of the ceremony—was left with her.

'Do you think he'll like me?' Zipporah asked the nurse nervously, only too aware how easy it was in her culture for a wife to be discarded by a dissatisfied partner.

'Of course he will,' replied the nurse, reassuringly. 'I'm

sure he'll think you are beautiful. Now come on—put this on! Moses will be here to collect you soon!' The nurse produced an intricately embroidered veil and threw it over Zipporah's head, covering her face completely.

Later that evening, Moses, wearing a special headdress and a garland of flowers around his neck, walked. to Jethro's tent accompanied by claps, cheers, music and dancing from the rest of his adopted clan. Dozens of lamps spangled the dark desert night. As he arrived the nurse lifted the heavy entrance flap and ushered Zipporah forward. Moses smiled, looked at her tenderly, and then took her arm and escorted her and her family back to his own tent for the wedding feast.

And what a feast it was! Several of the clan's precious lambs had been slaughtered and roasted on the fire, sending a succulent aroma wafting across the camp. The people tucked into their meal hungrily. Meat was a rare treat for a Bedouin, reserved for very special occasions. Their normal diet consisted mainly of cheese and bread.

The eating, drinking, singing and dancing went on for more than two hours and then eventually the steward of the feast called the festivities to order and the wedding ceremony began. Zipporah stood between her father and Moses, who took a special cloak and covered Zipporah with it, using the words, 'From now on, nobody but myself shall cover you,' a historic reference to the spiritual 'covering' that God expects a husband to provide for his wife even now, thousands of years later. Sometimes this ceremony was carried out by one of the bridegroom's relatives, but since Moses had none in this Bedouin clan, he performed it himself. There were claps and cheers from the couple's friends and family, who then gathered round and prayed for the newly-weds, speaking out prophecy and words of blessing and encouragement.

Moses and Zipporah bade their family and friends goodbye and at last they were alone together, to consummate their marriage and begin their lives together. Moses moved closer to her and slowly lifted up her veil so that he could see her face for the first time.

'In the name of God, the compassionate, the merciful, blessed be this night,' said Moses, gently.

'God bless you,' Zipporah whispered back, her head bowed. Moses then walked across the tent, pulled back the curtain and called out to the women standing outside. 'Yes, she pleases me!'

There were shrieks and shouts of delight outside as Moses went back into the tent to be with his teenage bride. This shout from a satisfied bridegroom was one of the most delightful sounds that could be heard in the Bedouin culture. Since girls above the age of puberty had their faces covered all the time by a veil, it was impossible for a suitor to know whether they were pretty or not until their wedding night. Some, like Jacob, got a nasty surprise when they found their brides were not all they expected them to be! But Moses had no doubts—Zipporah was as beautiful as he had hoped, and he loved her.

Outside, the festivities continued, as they would for several more days.

But one man had left the revelry and was standing away from the tents, gazing at the twinkling cascades of stars in the cool night sky. Jethro's brow was furrowed in thought. Like many fathers who had just handed over their daughters to be married, he was worried. It wasn't that he didn't like Moses—he loved him as he did his own son, Hobab. But Zipporah . . . marrying a foreigner . . . and a murderer, too? That was hard to come to terms with.

According to Bedouin culture, Zipporah would probably have been expected to marry her cousin. But Moses had thrown Jethro's plans for an arranged marriage into turmoil by asking to marry the girl himself. The approach was unusual, but not unheard of, and Zipporah had enthusiastically agreed to the proposal. Negotiations had then continued about the gift that Moses would provide for Jethro's family in exchange for the girl, a tradition which sealed the covenant of betrothal and bound the families together. Normally, the groom would buy the girl for around seven camels, but since Moses had no possessions of his own, it had probably been agreed that his gift would be to look after Jethro's flocks. Betrothal was as binding as marriage itself and once the covenant was agreed, the woman was under an obligation of faithfulness to her husband.

All the arrangements had been conducted very smoothly and a date was fixed for the wedding ceremony. But right through, Jethro had felt uneasy about the marriage . . . and he still did. Moses was very strong willed. So was Zipporah, and she had a fiery temper, too. And then there were the differences in their cultures—Moses had been brought up as a prince in the luxurious palaces of Egypt, whereas Zipporah was just a shepherd girl and knew no other life than the desert.

Jethro prayed for the newly-weds that night, and again the following morning, when Moses fulfilled the custom and presented him with a blood-stained cloth which was legal proof of Zipporah's virginity. Perhaps he prayed that God would bless them . . . and keep this headstrong couple together so that God's purposes for them both would be fulfilled.

Moses gazed across the blistering desert wastes and shielded his eyes from the glaring sun. He felt weary

. . . utterly exhausted. He thought back to the days when he had been a soldier leading Pharaoh's army. Tough times . . . but not as tough as now. He had never realised that a shepherd's job could be so demanding . . . and so thankless, so lacking in real reward. There were times when the afflictions of the desert were terrifying: the constant threat of animals, the scorching days when the water was scarce, his bottle was empty and his parched tongue stuck to the roof of his mouth.

But there were times of tremeandous fun and laughter, too, when Moses would break the lonely monotony by running away from his sheep and pretending to hide from them. Within minutes they would be chasing after him and would soon encircle him, a woolly mass of bleating and baaing creatures, eager to see their master again. But both during the good times and the bad times, three things dominated his thinking, the same as they dominated the thinking of any Bedouin shepherd . . . he had to feed the sheep, defend them and care for them, no matter what the cost. He literally had to die for them if necessary. It was an awesome job description, and yet that was the bitter reality for Moses the shepherd. And many thousands of years later, the terms and conditions haven't changed, whether you are looking after sheep and goats— or people.

For Moses and his clan, Jethro's flocks literally meant the difference between life and death as they pursued their simple lives in the desert. They had to look after them—or face poverty and possibly even death through starvation. For the desert often suffered years of sustained and relent-less drought, when the autumn rains came too late and were too weak to produce fresh green pastures. These were bleak, sometimes terrible times for shepherd famil-ies. The sheep and goats were not able to produce any young during droughts and if the rains stayed away for more than two years, most of the animals died.

But Bedouin families were hardy. They were used to the cruelty of the desert and when calamity struck, they simply started rearing their flocks all over again. They knew that in a good year, their flocks might give birth twice and treble their assets. If a family had two good years in a row, they were normally able to withstand the bad years.

The whole nomadic way of life revolved around providing the animals with their daily feed. This meant being constantly on the move, since there was never enough pasture to remain in one place for long. And so Moses and the rest of Jethro's clan would migrate according to a yearly pattern, determined by the changing seasons.

Their primary need during the summer was to stay close to the wells and springs which their ancestors had dug from the rocky soil and which were filled up with the winter rains. Then after the autumn rains they would move on to allow new grass and shrubs to grow ready for next summer. During the winter the water was normally plentiful and by the spring the pastures would be covered with a breath-taking tapestry of coloured flowers and some thin grass, ready for the sheep to eat.

Bedouins learned to survive on between four and twelve inches of rainfall per year—and over the centuries had discovered that water was a commodity that had to be shared. They relied heavily on wells, some of which were hundreds of years old. The deepest ones were covered by a massive stone, so heavy it could only be moved by several men. So there was no room for independence—a shepherd had to wait for his friends to help him move it.

The lessons that Moses learned under the furnace-like sun and during the bitter black nights would have gone deep into his heart. They laid a foundation that enabled him to become a caring and successful leader of men.

Let's have a look at some of those lessons, which have eternal implications for all of us who would dare to take up God's highest call and look after his sheep . . .

They are God's sheep

Moses would learn an important lesson by the time he encountered God at the burning bush—that the Israelites were *God's* people, and nobody else's. 'Remember,' he rather cheekily told the Lord (as if God was likely to forget!) . . . 'that they are *your* people' (Ex 33:12–13).

When we're busy looking after people, it's often easy to forget that they are God's sheep—not ours. We may be their pastors, leaders or house group leaders, but God is their Shepherd. Others may have certain influences on their lives, but men and women will ultimately have to be accountable to the Lord, and him alone, on judgement day. In the Old Testament, God was primarily known to his people as a shepherd (Jehovah-Raah). And Jesus is referred to as the Chief Shepherd several times in the New Testament (Heb 13:20, 1 Pet 2:25 and 1 Pet 5:4). Indeed, in some ways being a shepherd was his primary focus as he established his ministry . . . 'I am the good shepherd. The good shepherd lays down his life for his sheep,' he told his disciples in John 10:11.

Few people will dispute that our churches are made up of God's sheep. Caring for people in a way that actually models this is a lot more difficult! It's easy to give mental assent to the principle—and not live by it.

Nowadays, you often hear church leaders referring to 'my people' and saying things like 'I've got 200 people

in my church.' Maybe it's just the way they word it—but
it can be easy to lose sight of the fact that the people do
in fact belong to God—and God alone. There's no dual
ownership or dual allegiance. It's an important point,
because if any of us regard people as 'ours' rather than
God's, there's a danger we will start to play God to them
and take on a role in their lives that only God himself
can fulfil. Even the Creator of the universe respects our
dignity and our rights to choose and to disagree with him
and go our own way if we want to. It's unlikely that any
of us will set out to become 'gods'—but it can happen
unconsciously unless we make a disciplined effort to
avoid it.

The danger becomes greater when we are striving for
bigger churches. We subconsciously start playing the
numbers game, regularly totting up how many members
we've got, to see how we're doing. The underlying agenda
here can be that we're counting the sheep as ours . . . a
practice that earned David some divine discipline in
2 Samuel 24:1–17. It's not clear why God was so opposed
to David counting his armies, although I suspect it was to
protect him from pride. Now this is not to say that God is
going to punish us the next time we count the numbers in
our congregation! But the principle remains the same: if
we are pastoring people in the way we should be, we will
be more concerned with how they are, rather than *how
many* they are!

Jesus never went for numbers—quite the reverse, in
fact—he often seemed to preach to *reduce* his following
rather than increase it! On one occasion (in John 6) he
gave a talk about being the bread of life. 'This is a hard
teaching,' his disciples told him in verse 60. 'Who can
accept it?' And we're told a few verses later that many of
Jesus' disciples turned their backs on him and didn't

follow him any more after that. It was even touch and go whether the twelve would remain faithful.

And Jesus was fully prepared to let them go rather than compromise his message. He knew there was a factor that was more important than numbers: he knew that people ultimately belonged to his Father. That's why he was able to refer to his disciples as 'those whom you gave me' when he prayed for them in John 17. It was because of this realisation that he was able to balance his deep love for them with the ability to let them go their own way, as he did Judas and the rich young ruler.

If we recognise that people belong to God, we will develop an awesome sense of duty and responsibility and ensure that we never cross people's wills, deny them the freedom to choose, or demand submission from them. As Gene Edwards rightly states in his remarkable book *A Tale of Three Kings*: 'Men who harp on about authority have none. And kings who make speeches about submission only betray twin fears in their hearts: they are not certain they are really true leaders, sent of God. Men who don't have authority talk about it all the time.'

On the other hand, grasping the fact that people are God's sheep will give us a godly willingness to trust the rebellious and the double-minded into his care in situations when we have already gone several extra miles and have worn out our shoes!

The importance of the rod and the staff

As soon as Jethro appointed Moses to the job of tending his flocks, the first thing he would have done is equip him with a rod and a staff. These items were the primary tools of a shepherd's trade—and it should be no surprise to find out in Psalm 23 that God, the Great Shepherd, uses them too. But we should remember, as the shepherds did, that they were primarily instruments of *comfort*, not intimidation. Let's look at them one at a time.

The rod

It is interesting that in Jesus' prayer in John 17 he says that he *protected the disciples and kept them safe*. The shepherd used the rod—around two feet long, with a round or oblong head—to do the same. It had a loop round the handle, so that the shepherd could hang it on his belt, or pass it over his wrist during a fight so that it would not be knocked out of his hand.

The desert was a place of ever-present danger for the shepherd and his sheep. There weren't just wolves to contend with, but jackals, occasional leopards, shrieking hyenas, venomous snakes—and, of course, bandits. The shepherd's rod was his only source of protection, and was a lethal weapon in the hands of a brave, strong man. And he would have to be prepared to use it—and to die defending his flock.

It's easy for us to think that because we don't see wolves and jackals prowling the streets, we live in safer times. Quite the reverse is true! God's sheep are in just as much danger these days—in fact, more danger than in Old Testament days. In those times, the dangers were easy to spot. Now they're not. They are often subtle and unseen . . . the whispering lies and condemnation from demons, curses from occult groups, or the less dramatic-sounding but more insidious gossip that pollutes our churches and the apathy-inducing drip-drip of materialism. Are we prepared to die to save our friends—God's people—from these things? It might be that costly! And if we're not, we have no rights at all over that person, even if we do happen to be the bearer of a title. We should be prepared to be aggressive in our prayers and in our spiritual warfare in order to protect God's people—especially the new Christians, the young, the elderly and the unborn, all of whom face increasing and varied threats these days.

There's a strong trend among leaders nowadays towards delegating many pastoral duties and responsibilities. I'm not against this—anything is better than returning to the one man ministry where the minister attempts to do everything and ends up achieving nothing of value! Good delegation should improve pastoral care, as the Jerusalem church found in Acts chapter 6, where some simple restructuring ensured that some Greek widows received their daily share of food. And we shall see that Moses would learn from Jethro in this regard too. But in their enthusiasm to delegate, leaders should beware abdicating their duty to protect people and keep them safe. Jesus never delegated such important responsibilities. He delegated many things—preaching, performing miracles, deliverance, healing, administration and even looking after the money. But he *never* delegated his role as protector of his flock—and neither should a church leader. There is nothing that terrifies the enemy more than the leaders of a church standing up and, in Jesus' name, ordering him to get his hands off God's people! The enemy is a legalist and knows the lines of authority only too well. That's why he knows that if he can strike the shepherd, the sheep will scatter (Zech 13:7).

Two leaders who have made a deep impression on me are the late Metcalfe Collier, of Brigadier Free Church in Enfield, North London, and John Barr, of the Elim Church in Canning Town, East London. One of the many lessons they have both taught me is the importance of praying for every member of the congregation by name, on a regular basis. Metcalfe even had a card index containing the names of literally thousands of people he had prayed for over the years. The practice produces safe churches and we would do well to learn from it. If Jesus could find the time to pray for Peter by name, then we should be able to do the same for the people God has given us to look after.

The staff

The staff was a stout, wooden stick that was bent into a crook at the top. It would often last a shepherd a life-time—certainly Moses got good use out of his, using it not just to tend sheep, but to perform amazing miracles, to divide the Red Sea and bash the occasional rock to obtain water when the Children of Israel were thirsty!

Shepherds used their staff for two main purposes—to *guide* and to *inspect*.

Guiding the flock. Sheep and goats are notorious wanderers and one of the shepherd's main duties was to make sure they didn't go astray. He would often throw a stone in front of a wanderer, to frighten it back to the main flock, and on other occasions would use his staff to gently steer the wanderer back.

The risks were greater up in the mountains, where animals easily wandered too close to the edge of the narrow paths and fell into a ravine below. On these occasions the shepherd used his staff to hook the stray around the back legs and pull it back on the path. Sometimes a sheep got lost. Then the shepherd had to spend hours trekking through the wilderness and along desolate ravines until he found it. When he did he would carry the creature home on his shoulders and arrive back, exhausted and hungry.

God's humour in comparing his people with sheep often makes me laugh! I don't think he could have found a better comparison. Look around your church and you'll find the similarities are all too obvious. If one person does something—everyone else follows, whether it's prophesying in a certain way or reading the latest 'in' book. And there are still plenty of wanderers these days! There will always be people who are prone to wandering off into weird spiritual experiences, unreal faith, strange doctrines and bad company. A good pastor will make sure he uses his staff in the time-tested way—to guide, not to beat. It might be tempting at times to use it to hit someone over the head, and perhaps sometimes they might seem to need it! But that's not God's way, and should never be ours. I've sadly seen wanderers driven further away from the flock by heavy-handedness, when all they needed was a gentle nudge back in with a cup of tea, a listening ear and a shoulder to cry on. How sad—not just for the victim, but for the shepherd, too, who will have to give an account for that sheep one day, just as Moses would have done thousands of years ago.

It's easy to spot the wanderers. They either remain on the edge of the flock—on the edge in relationships, in activities, and sitting at the back in meetings . . . or are so zealously committed that they spend most of their lives living in spiritual strata that bear more similarities to the Starship Enterprise than everyday life! We should be actively seeking out both these groups of people and trying gently to bring them into the safety of the flock.

Examining the flock. In the deserts you regularly see the shepherd make each sheep pass under his rod as it goes in and out of the fold. He uses the rod to hold the sheep down gently and check them for infection and thorns. Ignoring these things could put the sheep's life in danger later on.

In churches, good shepherds know that both they and their people need thorough examination—both from God and from others. We need both: God to show us our hidden faults, and people who love us enough to speak honestly into our lives and tell us what we're really like and how we can change.

However, before we have this kind of input into someone else's life, we should remember two things. First of all, we can only speak into their lives if they give us permission—unless there's a sin issue involved. And secondly, we should always read the verse about treating other people as we would wish them to treat us before speaking into someone's life. The principle is important: if we're not prepared to hear it from someone, we shouldn't dish it out to them!

We all need God and other people to apply the rod of examination to our lives—and sometimes allow God to decide who is going to wield it!

The shepherd's voice

Over the years Moses' sheep would have learned to follow him, not because they had to, but because they recognised his voice—instantly. That's why there was little danger of them going off with a stranger. Sheep simply didn't follow strangers, because their voices were unfamiliar. That's the ultimate test of an anointing on a leader—whether or not they've got people following them. If they haven't, no title on earth will ever make them a leader. And you often find that those who are genuinely anointed with leadership authority are so unassuming it probably wouldn't occur to them that they had it. But the flock will recognise it every time.

Jesus spoke in John 10 about his sheep knowing his voice. The voice is a supremely important pastoral tool. Any leader who finds people are leaving his church would do well to ask himself: 'Do they really know my voice? And if they do, do they like what they hear?'

So much leadership is done by memo and fax these days, it's not surprising that the sheep doesn't recognise the shepherd's voice. His headed notepaper, maybe, but not his voice! We need to make sure that tenderly-spoken words, not pieces of paper, are at the heart of all our dealings with people.

Few of us realise the importance of our voices—and the words we use. If there's harshness or sarcasm in our tone, then it's unlikely that sheep will follow us for long. It's easy to claim to be speaking the truth in love and then walk over someone with our size tens and go off to our next meeting, leaving the victim wounded for months, if not years. I've known people leave churches and withdraw from ministry completely because of a couple of unkind sentences from one of God's people. Leaders have to take particular care with the things that they say—their words often carry more authority than they realise. The tongue has the power of life and death—and a shepherd who causes wounds with his tongue won't have sheep around for too long. A shepherd's words can literally kill people's ministries, their hopes and their relationships with God. But on the other hand all of us have a responsibility to treat our leaders with love, respect and kindness. There are very few of them who deliberately set out to cause hurt and get things wrong. And yet how many of them have been emotionally crippled by the things people have said to them, either one-to-one or in the 'safety' of the church business meeting?

I know one dear brother who actually died after being subjected to some of the most awful abuse and criticism from God's people. We all need to examine our speech carefully and ask for God to sweeten our hearts so that our words bring healing and not hurt. We need to beware making harsh judgements and rash promises, for these things can cause more damage than we could ever imagine. Gentleness is the key at all times: if we correct or advise with a harsh or bitter heart, then it won't be long before the sheep get hurt and scatter.

Silence is also a rare and valuable gift these days! We see in Isaiah 53:7 that Jesus was like a sheep that was *silent* before its shearers . . . he did not open his mouth. If only we could copy him at times! How often do we sound off with our judgements, words of wisdom and even prophecies when silence would have been far more helpful?

You normally find that churches which have not suffered splits and divisions are ones where the leaders are people who are kindly spoken and discreet with their speech.

The gate

Moses must have found that the shepherd's job was a torturous one at times. There was little, if any, shelter and the weather was often dreadful. The nights were bitterly cold and during the winter there was snow and frost to contend with as well. Rain and swirling winds often beat against the shepherd's face and then there were the floods and ferocious desert sandstorms. The shepherd would be desperate for sleep at night, but wouldn't dare to take the risk—the dangers were too great, and the sheep too valuable. He would literally guard the sheep with his life, sitting across the gateway to the fold, forming a human barrier to the wild animals, with only sheepskins and old rugs for shelter. A shepherd frequently suffered the agony of frostbite or of the skin peeling off his feet due to continued exposure to the vicious and unrelenting desert elements.

People who sat across the gateway to the fold had to be tough. They sometimes died.

'I am the gate for the sheep,' Jesus once told a group of Pharisees. 'Whoever enters through me will be kept safe. He will come in and go out and he will find pasture.'

But being a gatekeeper cost him his life. The Pharisees, along with other so-called shepherds who were more concerned with their position than their people and who used legalism and structure to avoid hard work, made sure of that. And yet, 2,000 years later, Jesus is still alive, and is the gate for the sheep. Or he should be. Sometimes these days he isn't. We need to ask ourselves: 'Is our evangelism leading people to Jesus—or to church?' The two should be inseparable, but sadly this is not always the case. If evangelism leads people to Jesus, they will generally become disciples, because if you truly meet Jesus, you cannot help but recognise your need for forgiveness and try to change your ways. If it leads them to church, they will become members . . . and perhaps enter God's kingdom by 'another way' (Jn 10:1).

A friend of mine used to have extraordinary success in leading people to Jesus by knocking on doors. Every Tuesday night, come rain or shine, he would go out and knock on doors in a selected road—and unashamedly talk about Jesus. No frills. No gimmicks. No leaflets about church or church activities. He simply told them about Jesus. And every Sunday he would bring the people who had entered the fold through the Jesus gate along to church. He knew the vital truth that the only way into the fold of God's kingdom is through Jesus.

Our churches don't always reflect this. We can often spend too much time in evangelism introducing people to the body—but not to the Head. And our churches are often difficult for a would-be sheep to get into. One person I counselled wanted to join a new church—and it was a good church, too. But after a few weeks, he gave up—on church and on God. Why? It was too difficult to 'get in' to the church. First, he found it difficult to find out where and when they met. And once he got there, he was confronted with forms to fill in and a course to go on to 'get in'. He wanted to have a chat with the man in charge, but he couldn't do that, either—there were tiers of authority, procedures to go through. He couldn't get in. So he got out. What a shame he wasn't introduced to Jesus, the accessible, welcoming gatekeeper, rather than a mass of structure and bureaucracy. He couldn't even meet the pastor.

In the Old Testament, the Children of Israel met with God in the tabernacle. And one striking thing about this awesome tent construction was its gate, or door. It was huge, around thirty feet wide . . . far wider than you would expect or than was strictly necessary. And the only barrier from going inside was a beautiful purple, blue and scarlet curtain—a curtain which did not need a key and did not need any strength for people to get through.

Are our churches as easy to get into as this? Are the gates effortless to get through? Or are they inaccessible, foreboding and difficult to penetrate?

If we keep Jesus at the centre of our evangelism and the gates to our churches wide and welcoming, we'll never suffer from a lack of sheep eager to go through them.

The importance of the new-born

Lambing was the happiest time of year for the shepherd—
and sometimes the saddest.

The lambs were born between January and the beginning of March, and it would be a frantic season with
dozens of new-born lambs to take care of. The ewes
gave birth to their young almost round the clock and their
offspring would need very special care for several weeks.
Sadly, though, many of them died, despite the shepherd's
care . . . sometimes through lack of food, or more often
because of the unpredictable spring weather. The frost and
snow and heavy rains took their toll.

Shepherds like Moses had to use all their skills to tend
the new-born lambs. There was so much to think of, and
you needed to be on hand twenty-four hours a day, for
weeks at a time. The pregnant ewes had to be driven
slowly, to prevent them becoming injured—for if a
mother sheep died, then its offspring would probably die
too. Isaiah captured God's heart in this . . . 'I will gently
lead the nursing ewes,' he said in chapter 40:11. And the
lambs had to be kept with their mothers in the pastures,
because the new-borns were too weak to walk far.

For this reason the shepherd carried them if it was
necessary to find fresh pasture. And as the lambs' legs
grew stronger, new dangers emerged. They were prone to
wander and, as they could not see very well, they had to be
stopped from eating poisonous plants.

It was always possible to tell a good shepherd by the
number of lambs in the flock which survived. It still is.

God has a similar concern for the new-born lambs of his
kingdom: that's why Jesus' first instruction when he
commissioned Peter was to feed the lambs. He recognised
that if you don't tend the lambs, you will one day end up

with no sheep at all. We need to ask ourselves whether we give sufficient priority to feeding the lambs in our modern churches—or whether it is the older sheep who receive all the quality input.

In Isaiah 40:11 we also read: 'He tends his flock like a shepherd: He gathers the lambs in his arms and carries them close to his heart.' That's God's nature—to carry the weak and helpless near his heart. As we seek to emulate him, we should do the same. Those new Christians might be demanding, they might be awkward and they will certainly be time-consuming . . . but spiritually they are weak and vulnerable. They cannot feed themselves, they may not be able to see clearly in terms of right from wrong or good and evil. And they are prone to wander. They must be carried—for as long as necessary. It's a thankless task, and not always an enjoyable one. It's easy to give our time and attention to people who are spiritual and mature, because we probably get built up from the relationship as much as they do. But true shepherds will always give the lambs the best attention. If they don't, the lambs will get devoured.

Happily, most churches are well tuned in these days to 'follow-up'. We are quite good at organising courses for new Christians. But these things are not enough on their own. It all comes down to heart attitude. We must be finding the good shepherds in our congregation—the people who can carry the sheep close to their hearts, who can protect them until they can see more clearly and are less prone to wander. It's the only place where they will be really safe.

7

A Man with a Calling

The sun crept up from behind the menacing highlands and stark ravines of the Sinai peninsula, its rays igniting a kaleidoscope of colour. In the bleak stillness of the dawn, Mount Sinai, known in the area as Jebel Musa, stood alone and apart from the other crags in this forbidding desert region, a majestic 2,600-foot mass of angular granite, its three peaks twinkling and sparkling in shades of violet, red, purple and grey.

Moses woke up and listened to the silence, just as he had done every day for the last forty years. Even after all this time, he still found it almost breathtaking . . . an awesome, sobering stillness that penetrated the mind and the heart louder than any crack of thunder ever could. It was a silence that enabled him to hear the still, small voice of God, who still woos us into the quiet even during the excitement and noisiness of his modern church.

Moses rubbed his eyes and climbed to his feet. The sun was already starting to bathe the plain with warmth and light and Moses was keenly aware of the need to press on with his journey. He was heading south, through Wadi

130

Nasb to the coastal village of DiZhav, where there would be plenty of pasture for his father-in-law's flocks. He wanted to get to the high inland plain of er Rakha as quickly as possible, since there would be enough grass there to sustain his animals for a few days before they embarked on the final leg of the journey to the coast.

Moses reached into his rough bag, took out some dry bread, cheese and dates and ate them hungrily, washing them down with a little of the precious water in his goatskin carrier. He knew only too well that water was a commodity which had to be used sparingly, since in the desert there were no guarantees of finding any more when you needed it and death through dehydration was an ever-present danger.

Moses called to his sheep, rounded them up and then slowly led them through the wadis towards the bottom of the great mountain, occasionally glancing back to make sure that none of the animals had strayed away from the rest of the flock. It was a routine that he had followed day in, day out, year in, year out for forty years in the shimmering furnace of the desert. Each day was the same, timelessly filled with simple, mundane tasks like caring for the sheep and looking after his wife and two grown sons, Gershom and Eliezer.

When the heat became unbearable Moses decided to follow the example of the flocks and rest in some welcome shade from an overhanging rock. He sat down on some soft sand, allowed himself another swig of water and looked across the flat plains that yawned out in front of him. Suddenly, something caught his eye. What was it? Yes, over there . . . a bush had caught fire. Moses looked away again . . . bushes often caught alight in the intense midday heat as the sun's rays magnified some of the quartz crystal lying on the ground.

A few moments later, though, Moses' eyes were drawn

back to the bush. Strange . . . it was still alight. Normally it would have burned itself to a pile of scorched wood and ashes by now. Moses was intrigued. 'I will go over and see this strange sight—why the bush does not burn up.' He clambered over the rocks towards the flames just yards away. Anything to relieve the boredom!

As Moses approached the bush, he was stopped in his tracks. The bush spoke! It called out his name, not once but twice. Moses hesitated fleetingly, thinking that perhaps the heat was playing tricks on his mind. But then he realised what was happening. This was God. It had to be.

'Here I am,' he said, tentatively, his voice faltering with fear.

The call to leadership

Moses did not know it at the time, but his conversation with God at the burning bush marked the end of another stage of his leadership training course. After forty years of disappointment, of hardship and of getting on with the everyday things of life, it was time to move forward! Moses, who had impetuously tried to deliver God's people in his own strength, was finally ready for a bigger challenge, but this time it would be on God's terms and in God's time, not his own.

We, too, need to know God's call to serve him . . . a time when he breaks into our mundane lives with a new commission and a fresh anointing. And there are some pointers from God's call to Moses which can help us recognise it when it comes to us.

1. God calls those who are busy already

God only calls people into leadership when they've proved that they can handle ordinary tasks. It's a principle that runs right through Scripture. Jesus confirmed it in Luke 16:10, 'Whoever can be trusted with very little can also be trusted with much.' Moses was a busy, hard-working man. He had proved to be a faithful and reliable shepherd over a long period of time. So had David—he too was busy tending sheep when the prophet Samuel sought him out and anointed him to be king. Gideon was busy in the winepress when God called him to be a mighty warrior. Peter was busy fishing when Jesus invited him to become a fisher of men. God's call always comes to busy people.

If we wait in the wings for God to call us to do something, we'll wait for ever. And every one of us can prove ourselves trustworthy with something, somewhere, whether it's putting away the chairs after meetings, looking after one or two people who need help or making sure the kettle's always on and the door is open to anybody who wants to call in.

So if you're frustrated in church life and wish you were doing more, simply do what comes to hand. Do it well, do it faithfully. Then you'll find that sooner or later, God will raise you up. And when he does, your character should be ready to cope with the tasks that he asks you to do. It's all part of God's leadership training programme.

It is also significant that God also calls people who are busy with what we would call *secular* employment. Even Jesus had spent at least a couple of decades working in the carpenter's shop before he 'went into the ministry'. This principle is important, especially for those who have dreams of working 'full time' for the church in some capacity or other. It is doubtful whether God will call us unless we have proved to him that we can hold down an ordinary job for a number of years. After all, how can a leader understand the pressures that ordinary people face, fitting in church activities with full-time jobs, if they themselves have never had to face them? Or how else can a leader keep in touch with issues like coping with foul-mouthed colleagues if they've never done it themselves? If leaders have not proved themselves in secular employment, they may end up making unrealistic demands on their people and being unable to counsel them on real-life issues with any authority. When Jesus said, 'Take the plank out of your own eye,' at least as a carpenter he knew what a plank looked like!

The apostle Paul is a good example: he continued with his secular employment (tent making) alongside his work for the church. This helped to keep his feet on the ground as well as providing him with a handy source of income. It's important that all full-time workers take every opportunity to keep in touch with the issues that ordinary people face—even if it means spending a week working at the burger bar during the holidays occasionally, just to find out what it's like!

2. We need to know God intimately

It's significant that when God called Moses at the burning bush, he called him by name. This implies that he and Moses had already built up a relationship with one another, one no doubt forged amid the silence and the pain of those years in the wilderness. Moses must have learned many lessons during that time, but one thing he certainly learned beyond doubt was to recognise God's voice. He had heard it before, probably in the stillness of his heart. That's why he was able to respond to it at the burning bush with little hesitation.

God calls all of us in different ways, at different times, to carry out different tasks. And we all need to know his voice so that when the call comes, we'll be able to recognise it and trust him sufficiently to obey it. If we

don't we might let an opportunity pass us by, simply
because we didn't hear it, or recognise it, when it came.

3. We need to understand the character behind the call

When God spoke to Moses, the first thing he did was to
reveal his holiness. 'Do not come any closer,' he told him.
'Take off your sandals, for the place where you are
standing is holy ground.' He gave these instructions
before he even told Moses his name! In other words,
what he was like took greater priority on that occasion
than *who he was.* There is an important reason for this.
God had chosen Moses for two main purposes—first, to
deliver his people and secondly, to make them holy, by
giving them the Ten Commandments and establishing a
priesthood. So it was important that Moses had a clear
understanding of a holy God right from the start, so that
the Jewish people would grasp the fact that the holy rules
were simply a reflection of the character of the God who
decreed them. This was why many of Moses' early
encounters with God involved fire, not just at the burning
bush, but the pillar of fire that led the Israelites through the
Red Sea and beyond and the smoke on Mount Sinai when
Moses met God and received the Ten Commandments.
Fire is symbolic of God's presence, his judgement and
his anger against sin . . . ingredients of God's nature
which the Israelites had to learn quickly after centuries
of living in the sin-stricken, multi-god culture of Egypt.

When God calls us, he will often give us a clear vision
of an aspect of his character which forms the basis of that
call. That's why he revealed himself to Abram as a God of
promises—because the rest of Abram's life would be
taken up with believing in those promises and seeing
them fulfilled. That's why he revealed himself to Samuel
as a God of judgement—because bringing that judgement,

first of all to Eli and then to the errant King Saul, would later form a significant part of his ministry. That's why God revealed himself to the boy David as a God of power—because David would see that power demonstrated on the battlefield time and time again in the years that lay ahead.

We will not be able to fulfil our calling unless we know the character of the God who calls us. After all, we're representing *him*, not ourselves, so we need to know what he's like. So we need to treasure the revelations of God's character which he gives us—not to the extent that we forget the other aspects of his nature, but certainly so that we can be confident that there is at least one area of God's heart which burns strongly inside us and equips us for the work we have to do.

4. We need to know the fear of God

It didn't take long for Moses to become afraid of God at the burning bush. 'Moses hid his face because he was afraid to look at God,' we're told in Exodus 3:6.

You don't hear much about the fear of God nowadays. There's plenty said about his fatherhood, about our rights to be his friends, and this is good, for we'll never really know him at all unless we can grasp these fundamentals. But we need to make sure that we learn to fear him, too, alongside these other characteristics.

I remember attending a church's morning meeting a few years ago. It was a hot day and the worship was at best lethargic. Most people remained in their chairs, singing the words of a chorus without much conviction. Then suddenly someone stood up and said, 'If the Queen of England was to walk through the door now, we would all stand up—immediately. We wouldn't even think about it. We'd do it out of respect. And yet when the King of

kings comes and stands among us, we don't even bother to
get out of our seats.' It wasn't long before everybody was
standing up!

It is easy to take intimacy with God too far, to the point
where we become matey and over-familiar with him. And
while thankfully the days are long gone where God is
portrayed by the church as a belligerent dictator who is
out to get us, we still need to remember that Jesus none the
less delighted in the fear of his Father (Is 11:3). Scripture
tells us that the fear of God helps us to obey his commandments (Jer 32:40), is the beginning of wisdom (Ps 111:10)
and the secret of leading an upright life (Ps 147:11). We
need to keep all of these things in mind as we seek to get
to know God better. Even though Moses had a face-to-face
friendship with God, he never lost that sense of fear and
respect for him.

5. We need to hear the call for ourselves

Significantly, the only person God spoke to about Moses'
call to leadership was . . . Moses. That's because he was
the person who would have to live with that call and the
burdens and pressures that went with it. If God calls us to
a task, it's absolutely essential that we hear the call for
ourselves. If we take on something just because someone
else has asked us to, told us to, or has given us a prophecy
about it, the chances are that we'll fail. Why? Because
when the heat is on and the doubts come, as they certainly
will, then it's only the word that God spoke to us that will
get us through. What he said to other people ultimately
won't help us. That doesn't mean to say that other people
won't be involved in that call. It's essential that they are—
after all the church is a body, a family, not a bunch of
Lone Rangers. The first thing Moses did after meeting
God at the burning bush was to go back and tell Jethro,

who gave Moses his blessing. The advice and opinion of other people are essential. But the call came directly to Moses.

There is a strong trend in churches nowadays for leaders to be raised up by other people, and this is a sound New Testament principle. But it's still important that those involved know that God has called them for themselves.

6. We need a healthy sense of inadequacy

When God explained to Moses what he wanted him to do, the best that Moses could manage was a list of rather feeble excuses, culminating with a pathetic appeal, 'Please send someone else to do it' (Ex 4:13). Compare this with the headstrong, over-zealous man who tried to take God's plans into his own hand forty years earlier!

It took God four long decades to break Moses' self-confidence and get him to the point where he was of any real use to him. And centuries later God chose a frightened, faith-renouncing fisherman with a tendency to chop off soldiers' ears when under pressure to be the leader of the first New Testament church!

I remember once attending a big celebration. The organisation was slick and the worship was as perfect as the musicians and the technicians could make it. At the end of the meeting the visiting speaker, a missionary from the Far East, asked three members of her own congregation to come and sing. They walked onto the stage, nervous and self-conscious, and proceeded to sing a song, quite badly, to the accompaniment of an out-of-tune guitar. In some ways, their performance was embarrassing to the sophisticated western congregation. And yet as they played, the power of God came down. People cried. Some were healed. Many gave their lives to God for the first time. It was an awesome display of God's power. That's because God still delights in using foolish things to confound the wise. He spoke to me clearly that night. He said, 'You live in a society which has made the church as good as man can make it. But a time is coming when the church will become as good as I can make it.'

While there's nothing wrong in being trained in our gifts and ministries, we must remember what Paul wrote in 2 Corinthians 12:9–10. 'My grace is sufficient for you, for my power is made perfect in weakness. Therefore I will boast all the more gladly about my weaknesses, so that Christ's power may rest on me. That is why, for Christ's sake, I delight in weaknesses, in insults, in hardships, in persecutions, in difficulties. For when I am weak, then I am strong.' And remember, this was the man who was surely one of the best-trained apostles there ever was. Like Moses, he'd had the best education and preparation available. But Paul had to come to a place where he saw it all as 'rubbish' (Phil 3:8) in order to be really effective for Jesus.

As Moses, Jeremiah and many other people found throughout the pages of Scripture, God is more likely to make effective use of the person who says 'I can't do it' than someone who says, 'Let me at 'em!'

The sun was a vivid fireball in the midday sky, but Moses was unaware of the heat. He was unaware of his thirst. He was unaware of the fact that the sand was starting to burn his bare feet. And for the first time in his forty years as a shepherd, he was even unaware of his sheep. He was a man alone with his God. To an onlooker he would have looked stupid, standing there talking to a blazing bush. But this meeting between the Creator of the universe and one of his beings was no ordinary encounter. It

had history at its heart. And when God speaks, nothing
else really matters. Our priorities are suddenly sorted and
we see ourselves as we really are. The Moses who stood
before God that day was pretty much like us . . . a
fumbling, fearful man who was full of feeble excuses. A
man, in fact, just like us. And there is a lot we can learn
from those excuses—and God's response to them.

He didn't feel up to the task

Perhaps God smiled when he heard Moses' first excuse.
'Who am I that I should go to Pharaoh and bring the
Israelites out of Egypt?' The man who had run ahead of
God's plans with hot-headed impatience was now reluctantly lagging behind! The man who had spent the first
forty years of his life in the Pharaoh's palace was now
scared to go back there! Now in a sense, Moses had a
point. Who *was* he to carry out such a mammoth task—
leading the biggest exodus of refugees in history? He was
right—he wasn't up to the task. But that's why God asked
him to do it—so that Moses would rely on God's strength
and not his own and so God alone would get the glory. But
God's response was very reassuring: 'I will be with you.'
Just five short words . . . but containing everything that
Moses needed to know. In effect, what God was saying
was, 'I'll be with you every second of every day, in every
problem you face, with every opponent you encounter, on
every mile of your journey.' And a read through the rest of
Exodus proves that God kept his word—he never left
Moses' side and was with the people of Israel day and
night, leading them, providing for them, and caring for
them for the next forty years.

God is still saying the same to us today, particularly
when we don't feel up to the tasks that he's called us to do.

His presence is just as constant and just as active. He wants to be just as involved in our lives as he was in Moses'. Sadly, most of us don't experience this because we don't expect it, don't think we deserve it, or sadly don't think we need it. The Israelites, under law and wandering in rebellion in the desert, experienced more of God's love and provision than many of us do under grace! They had shoes that never wore out, they were never sick, they had food provided for them every day and water whenever they needed it. We should expect the same kind of protection and provision from our God, who is still saying 'I will be with you' just as clearly now as he did at the burning bush.

He was afraid of rejection

Maybe Moses was still smarting from the brush-off he received from the two Israelites the last time he tried to deliver them from Egypt. He asked God, nervously, 'Suppose I go to the Israelites and say to them "The God of your fathers has sent me to you," and they ask me "What is his name?" Then what shall I tell them?' Again, Moses had a point—how could he explain a call from God to a nation of people who had grown up in a culture where all gods had names? What could he say to them that would convince them; that would make them listen to a stranger like himself?

Unsurprisingly, God had the problem covered. 'I AM who I AM,' he told Moses. 'This is what you are to say to the Israelites. "I AM has sent me to you."' It's important that we don't underestimate the significance of this short statement, for it was the first time in human history that God had referred to himself with a name which revealed something about his character. 'This is my name for ever,' he explained to Moses in Exodus 3:15. '. . . the name by which I am to be remembered from generation to generation.' However, even this revelation was bound up in mystery, for it is not possible to translate it accurately into English, or any other language, come to that. In ancient Hebrew, there are no vowels, and so scholars have suggested it sounded something like *Yahweh* (rendered *Jehovah* in some Bibles).

Up to this point, God was known simply as El, which means 'God', and Elohim, which in fact means 'Gods'—a hint of the Trinity, perhaps. Abraham used the word *Yahweh* at Beersheba in Genesis 21:33, when he planted a tamarisk tree and . . . 'called upon the name of the Lord'. And Jacob referred to him as *El-Elohe-Israel* (God is the God of Israel) when he built an altar to him in Genesis 33:20.

But all that changed on the shimmering day on the slopes of Mount Sinai, as God quietly ushered in a new era in human history. Now Moses would probably have heard the name Jehovah before, since it formed part of his mother's name . . . Jochebed meant 'Jehovah my glory'. But it was none the less the first time that God had used a name which described his character. In truth, no one really knows how to translate it, or whether they should even try to! The best translation links the word with the verb 'to be', and can be translated 'I am who I am', or 'I will be who I will be'. The statement implies that he is a God who doesn't change, who is present, eternal and self-sufficient. The word Yahweh strongly conveys a God who wants to act. So in effect God was saying to Moses, 'I want to be known as the God who is present and active.' However, accurate translation is still impossible, and the name is so holy that even today an orthodox Jew will not say it.

An encouraging factor in all this is that God was prepared to meet Moses where he was. Moses needed the reassurance of knowing God's name—and God obliged. There was no sense in which God insisted that Moses came up to his level. That's the way he is with us— always meeting us where we are, but loving us too much to leave us there for long!

God is still I AM today—he still wants to be present, eternal, self-sufficient and active in the lives of his people. As history unfolded, the number of his names increased to reflect more facets of his nature. We now know him as the Bread of Life, the Good Shepherd, the Rest Giver, the Provider, the God of Peace, the Healer, and many other things besides. All this means that God will be what we need him to be in any situation that we face in life—a healer when we are sick, a shepherd when we're weary, a provider when we're under financial pressure. What a tremendous God to worship!

He was worried that people would not believe him

Moses was racked with the same doubt that anyone faces every time they give a prophecy. 'What if the people do not believe me or listen to me and say "The Lord did not appear to you"?' he asked God in Exodus 4:1. Doubting God's voice goes back to the beginning of time, when the serpent deceived Eve with the words, 'Did God say . . . ?' And again, God was prepared to meet Moses where he was by displaying some spectacular supernatural signs to confirm his word. First, he told Moses to throw his staff on the ground. Instantly it changed into a serpent and Moses ran away from it—he had been in the desert long enough to know that you don't mess with poisonous snakes! But then God told him to pick the snake up by its tail, and as he did so it turned back into his staff again without

causing Moses any injury. In other words, God was saying, 'Do exactly as I tell you and you'll be fine. Run away
and you might get bitten.'

Now the significance of this miracle would not have
been wasted on Moses. He would have remembered, only
too clearly, that the serpent played a prominent part in
Egyptian worship and would have understood with confidence that his God was greater than any of the gods of
the New Kingdom. Reassuring stuff, when you are about
to go and confront Pharaoh and his magicians on their own
turf! And little did he know that the same staff would later
open the Red Sea, bring water from rocks and be raised to
defeat the Amalekites! There's a lesson here for all of us
who want God to use us to perform miracles. It starts with
using what's in our hands. For Moses it meant using a rod.
For us it will be something different, but it will be the
ordinary things that we do every day. It's the only place to
start functioning in the supernatural. That way, it is God
who is super while we remain natural.

The second miracle was equally significant. God told
Moses to put his hand inside his cloak. When he took it
out, it was covered in leprosy. Then God told him to put
it back again and when he withdrew it for the second
time it was normal once again.

In the desert culture leprosy was symbolic of sin, and
so in these brief few moments God gave Moses a lesson
on salvation which many people spend years getting to
grips with . . . simply that he *cleanses* sin and *heals*
sickness. It was the same message that King David
proclaimed centuries later when he sang about his God
who . . . 'forgives all your sins and heals all your
diseases'. It was the two-fold fruit of Jesus' death on
the cross which Peter explained in his first epistle . . .
'He himself bore our sins in his body on the tree so that

he might die to sins and live for righteousness; by his wounds you have been healed' (1 Pet 2:24). Forgiveness and healing have been God's dual promises to his people right through the generations and still hold good today— and yet we find it so much easier to have faith for forgiveness than we do for healing!

The revelation meant that Moses would never need to hang his head in shame for his sin any more . . . the murder of the Egyptian and all the things he had done wrong since then were now wiped away. He could stand before Pharaoh and look him in the eye with confidence, knowing that his past was dealt with for ever. And he knew he never needed to fear sickness again, a reassuring message for an eighty-year-old, which is presumably why Moses never died of illness. God simply took him to heaven and buried him personally!

Another reassuring aspect in this section is that God more than provided for Moses. He gave him a third miracle to keep up his sleeve in case the first two weren't enough to convince the elders of Israel. 'Take some water from the Nile,' he told him, 'and pour it on the dry ground. The water you take from the river will become blood on the ground.' Surely, this would have been the ultimate proof to any Israelite who still wavered in his belief in the God of Moses. The idea of the Nile's water turning into blood would have been a terrible omen, since the entire nation worshipped the great river as a god and depended on it for survival. And maybe Moses grasped the significance of the miracle, too—that the laws of sowing and reaping always hold good. The river that had consumed the blood of hundreds of Moses' peers would eventually spill blood upon the nation who perpetrated the murders.

In some respects, Moses was fortunate that God was so

quick and so generous in giving him these supernatural
signs. When some Pharisees and teachers of the law asked
Jesus for signs in Matthew 12:38, Jesus flatly refused to
oblige—and instead gave them a chilling warning about
his forthcoming death and resurrection and the judgement
that would follow it.

There is a reason for this difference in approach. God
will be only too ready to give a sign to someone who is
trying their hardest to believe and yet finding it difficult.
But he will not waste his time on providing one to convince a fault-finding sceptic, because miracles don't
always produce a change of heart. The people in the
village of Capernaum saw more miracles than the inhabi-
tants of any other town during the days of Jesus. And yet
Jesus pronounced woe and judgement upon them because
they refused to hear his message. He said: 'If the miracles
that had been performed in you had been performed in
Sodom, it would have remained to this day. But I tell you
that it will be more bearable for Sodom on the day of
judgement than for you.'

We need to remember this when we ask God for healing
and miracles as part of our evangelism. They don't always
produce a change of heart—and God will not perform
them to convince people whose hearts aren't right.

He wasn't any good at public speaking

You get the impression that Moses was scraping the barrel
when he got to his fourth excuse. While the first three
might have had some point to them, the fourth was more
the cry of a desperate man! 'O Lord, I have never been
eloquent, neither in the past nor since you have spoken to
your servant. I am slow of speech and tongue,' he pleaded.

Now it's hard to say whether or not this excuse was

true. It certainly doesn't sound like the man who had been educated in the fine Egyptian colleges and who used to be a statesman in Pharaoh's courts! But it doesn't really matter whether or not it was true. The point is that Moses believed it was true. How many times have you doubted you could do something, when everybody around you knows full well you can do it? It's so easy to be bound by the wrong perceptions we have of ourselves. Sadly, even God's assurance wasn't any help to Moses. 'I will help you speak and I will teach you what to say,' the Lord promised him. But Moses was still unable to trust God with his problem. So once again, God showed enormous patience and kindness and met Moses where he was. 'What about your brother, Aaron the Levite? I know he can speak well,' God told him. 'He is already on his way to meet you and his heart will be glad when he sees you. You shall speak to him and put words into his mouth. I will help both of you speak and will teach you what to do. He will speak to the people for you and it will be as if he were your mouth and as if you were God to him.' In other words, Aaron would do for Moses what God could—and would—have done for him!

However, although God was patient with Moses, he was also starting to get angry. We're told that his anger burned against him. Moses had said enough. At the end of the day, God was God and had to be obeyed. He had pronounced his call and there was no escape. Sobering stuff. Fearsome, in fact. But all part of God's nature if we really aspire to leadership. Although he will equip us in every way, ultimately he expects us to obey him. That's his right.

The voice of God stopped as suddenly as it had started and the bush no longer burned. For a while Moses simply sat there unseeing, unable to move, unable to speak, unable to think. A few minutes spent in the presence of God had left him exhausted . . . physically and emotionally drained.

A while later he rose unsteadily to his feet, his thoughts still a whirl as he tried to come to terms with what had happened. Had it been real? Yes, there was no question of that. But why him? It was hard to work it all out. Moses' mind reflected on the day when he had slain the Egyptian slave driver and had foolishly tried to deliver the Israelites on his own initiative forty years ago. The right thing at the wrong time and in the wrong way. But God had proved faithful. He'd stuck with him, believed in him, sorted out his character and then given him another go. But why? Moses didn't understand. However, as he started to round up his sheep again, his mind started to clear and he gradually realised that he didn't need to know why. God had called him and that was all that mattered. The rest was in God's hands. Confidence started to course through Moses' veins. Not a confidence in himself—that had long since melted away in the crucible of the desert. No, this time it was different. He felt a confidence deep inside . . . a confidence in his God, I AM. He must go and find Jethro!

The Moses who led his bleating sheep out of the wadi that afternoon was a new man.

How God tames the strong

God sometimes has to disable people in order to be able to use them. It's a side of his fatherhood that is not particularly pleasant, but it's a fact. He did it to Jacob, who had made a career of trying to make God's plans work on his own terms. God finally caught up with him, wrestled with him for a night and then injured his hip so badly that it left him with a limp. But at least that wounding encounter meant that Jacob was then capable of fulfilling God's promise to him of fathering a nation. Far better to walk with a limp than to miss out on God's best!

God did the same to the proud, self-righteous Paul. First of all he left him blind for three days; then later he rendered him vulnerable to a satanic messenger for the rest of his days. And he similarly disabled Moses, taking a man who was powerful in word and deed and reducing him to someone who apparently had a speech impediment and who was a mass of excuses and inadequacy. And there are others, too.

Why does God do it? Certainly not because he takes some kind of macabre pleasure in hurting his children. No, it's because some people are so strong, so talented, so able, that they are of no use to him—even though they might have a heart to serve him. The problem is that even though they want to serve God, ultimately they don't need him. They are strong enough and clever enough to fulfil his plans on their own. But God catches up with them in the end and often has to deal with them severely in order to release their true potential. It's not that their talents and strengths are of no use to him. That's not the issue. It's more that he needs people who are capable of trusting him and, more important, capable of obeying him.

To begin with, Moses wasn't able to do that. Nor was Jacob. Nor was Paul. But they all got there in the end, even though they all bore the disabilities of people who had battled with their God and eventually lost.

Fortunately, God doesn't have to disable all of his children. Some of us know from day one that we don't have what it takes to do the things that God asks us to do. But those strong men and women have to be tamed, they have to be broken, otherwise they will remain like wild horses—full of energy, but a danger to themselves and others.

Perseverance in prayer

Back in Egypt, the plight of the Israelites grew worse. The beatings became more savage, the deaths more frequent, the misery more intense. But little did the slaves know that their prayers and cries to God were about to be answered, at last. He had heard. He had remembered his covenant to Abraham, with Isaac and with Jacob. And he had become concerned and prepared to act. At last. Their perseverance had paid off.

In the book of Ezekiel, God is described as having four faces. These all give us glimpses of different aspects of God's character.

There's the lion—a fighter. There's an eagle—a God who soars in the spiritual realm. There's a man . . . indicating God's humanity, expressed in Jesus. And there's an ox . . . a good old plodder.

We all aspire to be like the lion and the eagle. But the ox? That's not so popular. For while some things in the kingdom of God, like deliverance, healing, being baptised in the Spirit, are instant, others take time. Things like getting prayers answered, dealing with character issues, sin habits and family problems all involve trouble and wrestling in prayer for long periods, and they are acutely painful.

It's only natural that we prefer the instant things and hope we'll avoid the painful matters. But as Christians who are hoping to mature in our faith, we have to learn to cope with both.

If we look at Jesus' life we see that he performed some remarkable healings and deliverances and miracles which were achieved in an instant. But he also spent tough hours in prayer, learned what it was like being under constant pressure, and had a lifetime of learning obedience through suffering. And the reason that both he and the early church saw such amazing things happen *instantly* was because they were prepared to spend time behind the scenes, wrestling with the devil, with God, and with prayer. It all comes down to perseverance.

What does that word mean? The Bible defines it as: adhering closely, continually waiting . . . persisting . . . continuing unswervingly. And whenever we read about perseverance in Scripture, it's usually in relation to prayer. In fact there aren't that many times in Scripture where prayer is mentioned in an instant context, much as we like to think otherwise. That's what it means to persevere: to stick in there, unswervingly and persistently. For God is not a God who needs to act in a hurry. His ways are not ours. He is a God who kept his people waiting hundreds of years in slavery before sending a deliverer to free them. We need to understand that when God is slow to answer, it doesn't mean he isn't going to answer at all . . . only that he hasn't answered yet.

So it's important not to be discouraged, distracted, or to give up.

As it says in Hebrews 12:1, we must learn how to run with perseverance the race marked out for us. That's the only way to real maturity.

8

A Man with Recognition

Jethro looked across the smooth, sandy slopes of the desert and rubbed his ageing eyes. Were they playing tricks on him? No, there they were . . . flocks of sheep and goats in the distance. Strange! Perhaps they belonged to another clan. Or maybe they were his? Surely not. Moses was taking them south to the coast. It would probably be months before he saw them again.

Half an hour later he looked up again. Yes, it was Moses. He would recognise that sturdy frame anywhere. Why was he coming back? He told one of his daughters to prepare a meal and sat down in his tent to wait and see why his son-in-law was returning so quickly.

As Moses drew closer, Jethro went outside the tent again and waved to him. Moses waved back. Jethro looked at him closely. What was it that was different about him? There was a peace about him that he had never seen before.

Jethro ushered Moses into the cool of his tent and they sat down and chatted as one of Jethro's other daughters prepared them some food and something to drink. After a while, there was a pause. Moses hesitated and then asked Jethro, tentatively, 'Let me go back to my own people in Egypt to see if any of them are still alive.' He didn't feel he could tell Jethro the whole story . . . the fact that it wouldn't just be a visit for old time's sake, but one that would eventually lead him into Pharaoh's courts and a situation of potentially life-threatening danger.

Jethro was silent for what seemed a long time. Deep inside, he knew the truth anyway. Ever since he had first met Moses, he had always known that the day would come when he would want to go back to his people. It was something Jethro had lived with from the time he had first taken Moses into his family, for he had recognised the hand of God on Moses' life. Who was he to stand in the way? He had to let him go and trust God with the rest. He looked up fondly at the eighty-year-old whom he had come to love so much and said, gently, 'Go, and I wish you well.'

The next day Moses gathered up some odds and ends for the journey, summoned Zipporah and his two sons and got his donkey ready. Jethro came out of his tent and hugged them one by one for a long time, tears streaming down his wrinkled, weather-beaten face. Then he watched as they trekked off into the distance, into the unknown, unsure whether he would ever see them again. And even when they were just tiny black specks on the vast, sloping desert horizon, he was still standing there, watching.

As Moses trudged along through the desert plains, he wasn't afraid of the mission that lay ahead. God had helped him overcome his fears by speaking to him again after the encounter at the burning bush. 'All the men who

wanted to kill you are dead,' he had told him (Ex 4:19).
That was good to know. At least there wouldn't be any
awkward questions about the murdered slave driver! And
then of course there was his staff, which he was clasping
tightly in his hand as usual. He had hardly put it down
since he had met God at the burning bush just days before.
It was more than a staff now. It was a symbol of God's
authority, of God's supernatural presence. When he held it
he felt reassured, confident in the fact that God would be
with him as he had promised he would be. No, he wasn't
afraid.

But he was worried. Worried about his wife, Zipporah.
Her agreement to obey God's call to go back to Egypt had
been grudging. It was a tough demand to make on her,
since she had never left the security of her own clan in
the deserts. And although she had agreed to join Moses on
the mission, it was clear she was not that happy about it.
And then there was her ongoing resentment about Moses'
demands to circumcise his son, Gershom. As someone
who was not historically a follower of God, she saw little
point in the ceremony and had expressed her views about
it strongly. She had reluctantly consented to their first son,
Eliezer, being circumcised but had put her foot down
when it came to Gershom. She and Moses had argued
about it time and time again and still the job was not
done. There had been times when the differences between
them were so strong and the arguments so fierce that
Moses had wondered if their marriage was all but over.
Divorce among Bedouins was easy—all he had to do was
send Zipporah back to her family and pay for the upkeep
of their children.

As Moses led his family in silence through the wilderness, a strange sense of foreboding came over him.
Yes, he was worried.

Moses and his family pressed on with their trek towards Egypt, following the trade route called The Way to Shur which ran from Beersheeba in the Negev desert, through the wilderness of Shur and into the northern Egyptian towns of Pithom and Succoth. It was a long, difficult journey, with the ever-present danger from bandits and wild animals, precious few oases and even fewer places to rest. However, after many days they arrived at an old stone lodging house which was often used by merchants and traders. Moses tied up his donkey and ushered his family inside. How nice it would be to sleep with a roof over their heads rather than spend another freezing night under the stars!

However, as the evening went on, Moses felt increasingly ill. He went and lay down on a rough stone bed as Zipporah made something to eat for herself and her sons. Sweat poured down his brow and he began to shake uncontrollably. His bones ached and the room began to spin before his eyes. He was violently sick several times and was not even able to hold down a few sips of water. Zipporah knelt by the side of his bed, mopping her husband's brow with a damp cloth. What was wrong? Moses, like other Bedouins, was rarely ill—even though he was over eighty, he was strong, agile and robust, quickly shaking off the occasional headache, cold and stomach cramp which afflicted all desert dwellers from time to time.

As the night wore on, Moses felt himself becoming weaker and weaker. It was as if his very life was ebbing away from him. He could scarcely speak. What was happening? Surely God would not send him on a mission to deliver his people from Egypt, only to have him die of a fever on the way? It just didn't make sense . . . but there again, nothing did as he lapsed in and out of consciousness, his delirious mind a complete whirl.

A while later, as he hovered on the brink of death, his thoughts suddenly became clear for a moment and he instinctively knew what was happening. This was God. It had to be. He had caught his attention through this sickness in the same way as he had done through the flames at the burning bush.

'What is it, Lord?' he rasped hoarsely, forcing out the words with the last dregs of his strength. His mind began to focus on the issue of Gershom's circumcision. So that was it! Moses realised that the illness must be due to his reluctance to carry out the ceremony.

He called out weakly to Zipporah and told her to go and get a knife—and her youngest son. She stared at him in disbelief and exasperation. Not this again! 'Do it now—go and get them,' gasped Moses. 'And then circumcise him. I can't do it. I'm too weak.'

Zipporah looked at him with contempt and did nothing.

'Do it,' Moses said again, fighting for breath. 'If you don't, I'll die.'

Zipporah hesitated and then reluctantly got up and summoned her son. Then she took hold of a rough flint knife and carried out the ceremony that had been instigated by Abraham hundreds of years before. After it was finished she picked up Gershom's bloody foreskin and touched it against Moses' feet in anger. 'Surely you are a bridegroom of blood,' she shouted at him and stormed off out of the room.

Moses' strength gradually returned and the fever disappeared. It wasn't long before he was able to get up and eat and he sat long into the night, thinking and praying. But eventually he made up his mind. He knew what he had to do. The following morning he ordered Zipporah and his sons to go back to Jethro. He would continue the journey alone. His family had to take second place to the will of

God this time. There was no room for further compromises. Eliezer and Gershom hugged their father briefly, but as Moses tried to kiss his wife goodbye she pointedly turned her face away and stalked off into the wilderness, not even turning back for a second glance at the man she had been married to for all those years. Moses sighed. Perhaps his marriage was over. The price of obeying God was certainly high.

Later that day he grimly pressed on with his journey, leaving the trade route and following an instinct to turn south back towards Mount Sinai once again—the same instinct that led Elijah back there centuries later after his showdown with the prophets of Baal. Little did he know that the Mountain of God was about to host another significant meeting—not with Yahweh this time, but with his older brother.

A harsh God?

To most of us, it seems rather harsh that God wanted to kill Moses just because he had overlooked an apparently unimportant matter like circumcision. It seems a bit like God attempting to kill a church member for not getting baptised!

But the issue here was not just one of circumcision. There were other serious factors involved.

The cost of obedience

Moses had an unfortunate tendency to do his own thing, even after decades in the wilderness being humbled and dealt with by God. It was the same headstrong attitude which he showed when he killed the slave driver forty years earlier. And if Moses was to succeed in God's mission to lead the Israelites into freedom, then he had to learn obedience—or fail. The risks were too great and the stakes too high to have a leader who was not capable of submitting to God in every area of his life. As Jesus said centuries later, 'From everyone who has been given much, much will be demanded; and from the one who has been entrusted with much, much more will be asked!' (Lk 12:48). God had given Moses an enormous job to do and expected obedience in return. Nothing else would do. There was no way that Moses could be trusted to lead God's people, and expect obedience from them, if he wasn't able to obey God himself.

God was not playing games with Moses in that lodging house. He wasn't taking part in a divine episode of *Call My Bluff*. Had Moses not finally fallen into line and had Gershom circumcised, then God would have taken his life and raised up another deliverer for his people. Moses' preservation at birth, the years of preparation in Pharaoh's courts and in the wilderness, the burning bush . . . they would all have been in vain, because when God calls someone into a ministry, that call only lasts for as long as they are obedient. God can remove the anointing whenever he likes—Saul is an example of that. He owes us nothing and we kid ourselves if we think we are indispensable in any way.

God still insists on his people, and especially his leaders, maintaining day-by-day obedience and the very highest moral standards in their lives. Leaders who are truly obeying God do not normally have much trouble in receiving obedience from their people. Perhaps that's why Moses never succeeded in getting the Israelites to submit completely to his leadership—because he never submitted completely to God's?

The importance of a well-ordered family

There was a glaring family issue in Moses' life that had apparently not been resolved. He had allowed Zipporah to come between him and his responsibilities to God. He was bowing the knee to her instead of to God. No wonder God had to bring the issue to a head! There was no way that Moses was in a position to take on the leadership of a nation when he was not able to lead his wife into doing the will of God over a fairly basic issue like circumcision. It was a serious problem that required radical action.

In his first letter to Timothy Paul makes it clear that a leader must have his home life sorted out. 'If anyone does not know how to manage his own family, how can he take care of God's church?' he asks (1 Tim 3:5). God was unable to allow Moses to continue in his ministry while issues at home remained undealt with. The family has always been the crucible where God has required us to work out the nitty-gritty of our faith, and if we can't establish his kingdom there, then we can't establish it anywhere.

Compromising to our partners

The main reason why Moses disobeyed God over the issue of Gershom's circumcision was to keep the peace with Zipporah, who was clearly unhappy with the ceremony. When the chips were down, God wasn't Moses' Lord—Zipporah was. Compromising to our partners is still a common problem in churches today and is one that applies to both husbands and wives. It's so easy to back down over what God has told us just to get a bit of peace and quiet at home. I've lost count of the number of leaders' meetings which I've attended where everyone was in complete agreement over something that God had said—only to find people doing a 180-degree turn overnight after talking to their partners about it! This isn't to say that our partners will not have a valuable role in helping us hear the word of God in situations, and in weighing it up. But there's all the difference in the world between reaching a decision before God, and back-tracking on what God has said because our partner disagrees with us. Husbands, as head of the household, need to be loving and clear when hearing God on behalf of their families . . . and then need to have the backbone to see the decision through.

Circumcision and obedience—the same thing

Circumcision can be traced back to the very beginnings of God's dealings with his people. He told Abraham that it was a symbol of the everlasting covenant between him and his people. But the practice was more than just a messy and painful physical process. It symbolised a cutting away, or separation from sin and unholiness. People who were circumcised were expected to demonstrate their covenant relationship with God by their obedience. 'Walk before me and be blameless,' God told Abram before explaining the ceremony to him. It was an outward sign of a particular lifestyle.

Although in the New Testament the practice was gradually discarded after some fierce disagreements between the pro- and anti-factions, God still requires absolute obedience from us. 'If you break the law, you have become as though you had not been circumcised,' Paul told the Romans in 2:25. And he reminded the Corinthians (1 Cor 7:19): 'Circumcision is nothing and uncircumcision is nothing. Keeping God's commands is what counts.' So the heart of the ceremony remains unchanged . . . obedience is the proof of the fact that we're covenant children of God. If we don't obey him, then we need to ask ourselves some straight questions as to whether we have been truly cut away from our old lifestyle.

God also made it clear to Abram that any man who was

not circumcised would have to be ostracised from his people because the covenant had been broken. Moses would have known this. Clearly God could not let him assume leadership when his son was a walking example of a covenant-breaker!

The fear of God

Even though we do not know for certain that God tried to take Moses' life through sickness, as I have assumed here—he might have done it another way—another question remains. Why did God feel he had to *kill* Moses in order to get him to obey him? A God who tries to kill his children because of their disobedience doesn't fit in too well with our modern concepts of his fatherhood! Surely God could have dealt with the issue in another way?

The point here is that Moses needed to *maintain* the fear of God which he first learned at the burning bush. Although that was a very significant encounter, it evidently was not sufficient to get Moses to carry out that little ceremony on Gershom! So he needed a fresh revelation of God's fear to keep him on his toes. So do we. Most of us regularly pray for a fresh revelation of God's love. But how often do we pray for a fresh dose of healthy fear? We all need a constant revelation of all facets of his character in order to live the lifestyle and enjoy the relationship with him that he wants us to have.

The fear of God is sobering and there are important lessons for us to learn about it, especially in this age of grace and effortless forgiveness. For even though God is a loving and forgiving Father, he is also a God who does not change. His serious side, manifested frequently in the Old Testament, has not disappeared! He is still a God of judgement. He still disciplines us and, according to Hebrews 12:11, that discipline is not pleasant, but painful. He will often use sickness to catch our attention. And he expects us to obey him, since obedience has been a requirement on his people since the Garden of Eden. This shouldn't be daunting. Under the New Covenant obedience should be a gift, not a burden (Jer 31:33 and 32:40)— something which we should exercise happily, knowing that if we do, God will bless us all the more.

In an age of grace it is easy to run away with the idea that God will bless us whether we obey him or not. While it may be true that his blessings are not conditional on our behaviour—it wouldn't be grace if they were—it is important to remember that a life of obedience will always produce more good fruit than a life of rebellion.

The Spirit that brings death?

Most churches nowadays have a real desire to move in the kind of power that the Jerusalem church saw in the book of Acts. But are they prepared to see Acts-style judgement, too? Pentecost power is accompanied by Pentecost purging, as Ananias and Sapphira found out to their cost! How would you feel if people were carried out of one of your meetings feet first, leaving you to explain the situation to their families, the wider congregation and the press? We must never forget that the God who tried to kill Moses is still alive and well. Although he is rich in mercy and slow to anger, that doesn't mean to say that he will never get angry and bring judgement to situations when they warrant it. That's why Peter warns us: 'It is time for judgement to begin with the family of God' (1 Pet 4:17).

A lesson learned

One thing is for certain: God taught Moses a lesson that he never forgot. He went from being someone who wouldn't circumcise his own son to become a leader who was an enthusiastic and diligent enforcer of the practice. In fact Jewish people later associated circumcision more with him than they did Abraham, who introduced it in Genesis 17:11. At the Council of Jerusalem (Acts 15) the pro-circumcision faction of the New Testament church twice referred to the ceremony in connection with Moses, and in John 7:22, Jesus had to remind the crowd that the practice went back to before Moses' time. 'It did not come from Moses but from the Patriarchs,' he told them.

It took Moses many years to obey God and circumcise Gershom. His failure to do so wasn't due to ignorance—he must have known the commands which God gave to Abram. And Moses had probably been circumcised himself by his parents when he was a baby. But he was slow to learn. He procrastinated and dithered. But he got there in the end.

The apostle Peter was another slow learner. Even though Jesus made it clear to him in the Great Commission that the gospel was for both Jews and Gentiles, it still took a rooftop revelation from God around eleven years later to get him out of his Jews-only mindset. And even then, he backtracked. As Paul neatly puts it in Galatians 2:12 'Before certain men came from James, he [Peter] used to eat with the Gentiles. But when they arrived he began to draw back and separate himself from the Gentiles because he was afraid of those who belonged to the circumcision group.' But despite his slowness to change, Peter got there in the end.

Men like Peter and Moses give us hope when we are so frustratingly slow to learn God's truths. God perseveres with us, for years if necessary, until the penny drops. But once it does, the lessons we learn last for eternity.

In a hut back in one of the Hebrew slave colonies in Egypt, an eighty-three-year-old man woke with a start. What had woken him? A voice, yes, that's what it was. He looked around the hut in bewilderment. Everyone else seemed to be asleep. Who had spoken?

Suddenly the voice spoke again. 'Go into the desert to meet Moses.' The man trembled and knelt down by his bedside. Surely this was the voice of God . . . the God who had not spoken to his people for hundreds of years now.

After a while Aaron stood up and collected his thoughts. Moses? Surely he was long since dead. He had grown up knowing that he had a younger brother who had gone to live in Pharaoh's palace. He had often felt jealous of him, living a life of luxury while he and the rest of his family were left to be beaten and abused as slaves. Sometimes he had scrutinised the royal processions as they passed by and wondered if Moses had been among the mighty men sitting regally on board the chariots. He had often heard stories about this successful brother of his, but then one day someone told him that he had killed an Egyptian and had gone on the run. That was more than forty years ago and nothing had been heard of him since. Aaron had assumed that he had died long ago. But now there was this voice, the voice of God perhaps, telling him to go and meet Moses in the desert!

Aaron stroked his beard thoughtfully and decided what to do. Yes, he had better go—but where? The desert was a big place—thousands of square miles of sandy and rocky terrain. What chance was there of finding Moses there? He would simply have to trust God.

Several weeks later, as Aaron walked falteringly across the plains at the foot of the saw-toothed Mount Sinai, he spotted a figure in the distance. His heart leapt. It had to be

Moses! A new surge of strength coursed through his aching body as he walked the remaining yards towards the man whom he hadn't seen for almost eighty years. As he drew close, Moses turned to him and they stood and gazed at one another briefly before embracing and kissing one another fondly. Introductions weren't necessary. Both men instinctively knew who the other was. Moses had been expecting the visit ever since God had told him about it months earlier. He ushered his brother to the cool spot where he had sat and watched the burning bush just weeks earlier and gave him some water out of his bottle. After a while they began to talk. There was an awful lot to catch up on.

Family reunions

We can only guess at the conversation that took place between Moses and Aaron that day. We know from Exodus 4:28 that Moses told Aaron everything that God had told him to say about the mission that lay ahead. And we know that he described the miraculous signs which God had commanded him to perform. But there must have been a lot of other things to talk about . . . eighty years' worth of family news, for a start! It must have been an emotional time for them both.

God loves family reunions. The Bible recollects many of them . . . hugs and kisses between Jacob and his uncle Laban when they met in Genesis 29:13; more of the same, with tears thrown in, when Jacob finally made up with Esau (Gen 33:4), and similar scenes when Joseph was reunited with his father and brothers (Gen 45:2–1 and 14). This is because God loves united families. It breaks his heart when they separate and it moves him to tears of joy when reconciliation comes. The story of the prodigal son shows how he feels when families are made complete again.

In the cases of Moses and Aaron and Joseph and his brothers, it was God who orchestrated the reunions. He is good at doing that, because he knows where people are even when they don't know where to find each other.

He did it for a friend of mine. She lost touch with her brother when they were both young children. They were farmed out to different adoptive parents and did not see one another for years, or have any idea where the other was. But my friend started praying about it. One day a man—a minister, as it turned out—spotted her reading her Bible on a train and invited her along to his church. She agreed to go—and when she got there she met up with her brother again! What a reunion that was!

God is also good at sorting out marriages—even when they're completely finished. Another friend of mine walked out on his family and went to live with another woman. He divorced his first wife and eventually married the other woman. But God eventually spoke to him in the same way as he did Moses—through illness. His second wife eventually left him and he became a Christian. Later on he divorced his second wife and remarried his ex-wife and they are still together, leading a church.

We live in a society where families are being ripped to pieces by sin, circumstances and the devil. Many people have long since given up praying for reconciliation. And many children don't know either who their parents are, or where they are. But there's always hope, because we have a God who is a reconciler, a uniter. If he managed to link up Moses and Aaron after eighty years, when they were living in different lands hundreds of miles apart, perhaps he can do it for you.

Moses and Aaron sat talking late into the night, keeping warm together beside a crackling fire. High above them, millions of stars cascaded through the heavens, and around them animals shrieked and howled. A bonding of true friendship had grown between the two old men as they chatted over old times and discussed the mission ahead. Moses gradually came to realise that he couldn't manage it without his older brother. The man who thought he could take on the job of deliverance on his own had finally learnt the lesson that we all need to learn if we are going to succeed for God . . . that God is into team-work and always has been.

God himself is a team—Father, Son and Holy Spirit, all with different roles and responsibilities, each loving and honouring one another. And he repeated the pattern when he recognised that Adam could not manage on his own and set him to work in team with Eve.

Right through Bible history, we find that the people who acted independently failed in the end. Samson, Saul, Absalom, Solomon . . . they were all loners who knew God's anointing and saw his power and his glory, but ended up in a mess because they acted alone.

When Jesus began his ministry, the first thing he did was establish a team. And he drilled his disciples on the importance of inter-dependence right from the word go. He always had them functioning in groups, or at least with a partner, whether it was ministering in the supernatural or doing basic administrative tasks like finding a donkey for the triumphal entry or booking a room for the last supper. The only disciple who acted alone was Judas. He was solely responsible for looking after the money, and it wasn't long before his independence gave Satan a foot-hold in his life . . . a foothold that enabled Satan to influence him to murder his Messiah. Independence

always produces death in the end. It did with Moses . . .
and it took him forty years to realise that he needed a
partner and he ended up with a dynamic working relationship with Aaron. While they were working in team, they
succeeded. But when they acted independently, problems
arose . . . as Aaron discovered when he tried to take on the
leadership mantle on his own with disastrous results while
his younger brother was up on Mount Sinai (Ex 32:1–6).

There are lessons here for all of us. Jesus taught us to
pray *Our* Father, not *My* Father, because he wanted us
to understand that while we are all called to have a
personal relationship with God, it will not flourish on its
own for long.

The meeting was hushed in expectation. The elders of the
twelve tribes of Israel sat in a semi-circle on the floor of a
disused hut while a younger man kept watch for Egyptian
soldiers outside. Their meeting was tantamount to treason
which was punishable by death. The elders, around
seventy of them, looked at Moses and Aaron with a
mixture of suspicion and curiosity. Aaron . . . yes, they
had known him, his wife Elisheba and their four children
for many years, and trusted them as godly people. But
Moses? He was an unknown quantity. They knew he was a
Hebrew by birth and stories about his successes and
exploits as a prince in Pharaoh's court were still legend
in their community. And they had heard about the incident
where he killed the Egyptian slave driver forty years
earlier. That story was well-known in their community,
too . . . the man who had the audacity to leave the luxury
of royal palaces when it suited him and had tried to set
himself up as their leader, without even asking the elders
of the time what they thought about it. The people had

treated him with the contempt he deserved. But what had he been doing all these years, especially when most people, including his own family, had given him up for dead? And what did he want with them now? Power? Position? To use them for his own political ends like before? Yes, they were suspicious, and they had every right to be. No man had the right to live life to the full in the palaces of their oppressors one day and then walk in and suddenly expect their allegiance the next. They looked at him guardedly, wondering why they were there.

Moses sensed their caution and felt nervous. The words 'Who made you rule and judge over us?', uttered by his countrymen all those years ago, still haunted him. Would the elders of Israel give him the same treatment and reject his second attempt to become their leader? Even though God had given him many assurances, he still felt unsure. He grasped his staff tightly and studied the elders carefully. They were a sad assembly: thin and emaciated, their faces haggard, their hair and beards matted, their clothes tattered and torn. But it was more than that. It was their eyes. They were dead . . . without sparkle. They were men without hope, representing a nation without hope . . . a nation who had called out to their God to deliver them from slavery for centuries but who had only seen their situation get worse. Moses felt an overwhelming sense of love for them. He knew what it was like to live without hope. And he was confident that with God's help, he could bring them into freedom. But would they let him?

Aaron stood to his feet and began to speak. A quietness came over the assembly and the elders began to listen as he eloquently told them about Moses, about his years in the wilderness, about the burning bush and about God's call to him to come and lead them out of Egypt and into a land of their own. The men listened carefully, weighing up

what was being said. Yes, it had the ring of truth about it.
And yet . . .

Aaron continued, 'God understands that you may find it
hard to believe what I am saying. But he has told me to
show you these signs. They will demonstrate God's concern for us and his power to help us.' Aaron reached out
for Moses' staff and hurled it to the ground. There was a
gasp as it turned into a snake and some of the men leapt to
their feet and ran towards the door. 'Wait!' Aaron told
them. And he reached and grabbed the snake by its tail and
it turned back into a staff again amid sighs and exclama-
tions of amazement.

Then Aaron demonstrated the second sign, placing his
hand inside his coat. There were cries of shock as he
withdrew it, disfigured by leprosy. But as he put it back
in and withdrew it a second time, completely restored, the
elders were convinced. Without any prompting they fell to
their knees and worshipped God, with tears and loud cries
of praise and gratitude . . . worship from the heart that had
not been seen in their community for centuries.

Aaron and Moses joined them. Moses was weeping, too,
as he bowed before Yahweh. Things had come full circle.
He had finally been accepted by the people who had
rejected him all those years ago. It was too awesome, too
incredible to grasp. God had made his dreams come true.

The words 'Who made you ruler and judge over us?'
came back to his mind again. Well, God had now put him
in that position, in his own time and in his own way. He
had put this headstrong young man through his own
leadership training programme . . . a programme invol-
ving pain, failure, loneliness and a tedious process of
redemption. But at the end of it he emerged as the hum-
blest man on the face of the earth.

9

A Man Dependent on God

The messenger looked around in utter amazement as he stumbled wearily through the Israelite encampment on the plains at the bottom of Mount Sinai. He had never seen anything like it before—a teeming hubbub of over half a million people, camped incongruously in the desert. There were men talking animatedly to one another, babies shrieking, children chasing one another through gaps between the animal-skin tents, and women cooking over open fires. The din, a stark contrast to the silence of the desert, seemed to pierce his eardrums. He wrinkled his nose at the stench of animal excrement and pressed on with his mission. He had been travelling a long time—weeks now. But he had finally arrived. And he had to find Moses.

'Why do you want him?' rasped an elderly Jewish man suspiciously. 'What's he to you?' The camp was still recovering from a recent battle with the King of the Amalekites—a spectacular triumph, but a costly one. Many men were still nursing wounds and were jumpy at the presence of a stranger in their camp.

The messenger spoke nervously. 'I am bringing word from Jethro, his father-in-law.'

The messenger was escorted to Moses' tent where he delivered his news. Jethro was on his way to meet Moses—and was bringing his wife Zipporah and their sons Gershom and Eliezer with him. Moses' heart missed a beat. He had never forgotten his family, but he had felt them slip to the back of his mind amid the excitement of the confrontations with Pharaoh, the plagues and then the incredible Exodus from Egypt. He felt delight tinged with anxiety at the prospect of seeing them again. He and Zipporah had not parted on good terms, but he had none the less missed her and was especially sad that she had not been there to share in his triumphs over Pharaoh. When his older sister Miriam had led the women of Israel in singing and dancing on the banks of the Red Sea, Moses couldn't help thinking that Zipporah should have been there too, joining in the celebrations.

They arrived several days later. Moses was summoned from his tent, went out into the blinding sunshine and prostrated himself before Jethro—a mark of deep respect and humility, the sort of gesture normally used before royalty or God himself. Then he went and kissed the wise old shepherd who had become a father to him over the years, his eyes filled with tears of pleasure at seeing him again. And it wasn't long before they were talking incessantly, following the Bedouin custom of asking interminable questions about one another's health and general well-being.

Moses went and greeted Zipporah and his two sons warmly, but still sensed some coolness in their response. Perhaps Moses later lived to regret the fact that Gershom and Eliezer never played a significant part in Israel's future. Perhaps that was the price he had to pay for marrying someone who was not a Jew, for she is described as a Cushite (or Ethiopian) in Numbers 12:1. Or maybe his sons were among the first children who found it hard to walk in the footsteps of fathers who had major ministries. They certainly weren't the last!

After a while Moses ushered Jethro into his tent and spent several hours telling him about the things God had done to Pharaoh and the Egyptians and how he had delivered the Israelites from all kinds of hardships.

Jethro sat and listened, his face a picture of delight and sheer amazement. And when Moses finally brought his story up to date with a graphic account of the battle with the proud King of the Amalekites, Jethro sipped some wine, shook his head and simply said, 'Praise be to the Lord. Praise be to the Lord, who rescued you from the hand of the Egyptians and of Pharaoh, and who rescued the people from the hands of the Egyptians.' He sat in silence for a while and continued, 'Now I know that the Lord is greater than all other gods, for he did this to those who had treated Israel arrogantly' (Ex 18:10–11).

That phrase 'now I know' is often used in the book of Exodus, presumably because Moses and the people of Israel were in a process of getting to know God in a significant way for the first time. *Knowing* him was important—knowing his ways, knowing his acts of power, knowing his character. And now Jethro, who had known God for most of his life, was getting to know him better through Moses' exciting testimony. And that *knowing* helped him worship him.

Knowing God is still just as important for us. And God will use all kinds of circumstances, both good and bad, to show us his greatness and to reveal his character to us. And we will find that knowing him will help us worship him, too.

Later that day Jethro and Moses stood around a fire
which was crackling dryly in the dusk. 'We should offer
sacrifices to the Lord,' Jethro said to Moses. 'He has been
good to us.' Moses nodded in agreement. Jethro didn't
know it, but he was inadvertently putting the seal on
Moses' mission out of Egypt. Moses recollected his first
tense meeting with Pharaoh. 'The God of the Hebrews has
met with us,' he had told him (Ex 5:3). 'Now let us take a
three-day journey into the desert to offer sacrifices to the
Lord our God.' Moses smiled as he realised that the
request was about to be completely fulfilled. The sacrifices were about to be offered—the first recorded occasion
since Jacob offered them at Beersheeba, when he was
fleeing Canaan to escape the famine hundreds of years
earlier.

After a while Jethro and Moses, helped by some of the
elders of Israel, had rounded up some male oxen, sheep
and goats and ushered them away from the other animals
into a special fold.

By now the fire was burning fiercely and dozens of
people, including the elders of the twelve tribes of
Israel, had gathered round, watching in reverence.
Silence fell as Jethro entered the fold and then held both
of his hands in the air. He was wearing a long, brightly
coloured *kufiyya* (head dress) which he only wore for
thanksgiving feasts, and carried a long knife in his right
hand.

'Let us give thanks to El Elohe,' he cried out. 'He has
protected you and delivered you from the hand of Pharaoh
and the Egyptians. He has brought you out of captivity . . .'
There were cries of gratitude from Moses and other elders
as he continued with his prayer. After he had finished it he
reached for his knife, grabbed a struggling animal, placed
his hands on its head and then slit its throat. Blood spurted

out, but Jethro, experienced with animal sacrifices, deftly caught most of it in a bowl. Once the animal was dead he and Moses skinned the carcass and divided it up, washed the legs and the entrails with water and then laid it all on the fire and watched until it was completely consumed by the roaring flames. It was a messy, smelly and time-consuming job, but one which was important because it was a way of saying thank you to God, just as Abel had done (Gen 1:4) when he had made the first animal sacrifices ever recorded in Scripture.

It is significant that it was Jethro and not Moses who carried out the sacrificial ceremony on the slopes of Mount Sinai, since it confirms once again that Jethro had a relationship of some sort with Yahweh, despite the fact that he is described as a Midianite priest, and not a priest of God. There is still a degree of debate about the real extent of his relationship with God. Some people believe that Jethro introduced Moses to God, while others think that it was the other way round, using Jethro's words 'Now I know that the Lord is greater than all other gods' as proof of the fact that Jethro did not in fact know God personally until Moses witnessed to him that day when they were reunited in the desert. My view is that Scripture leans towards the first view—and I find it fascinating that God may have used someone who *wasn't* one of his chosen people as a catalyst in a chain of events which climaxed in the deliverance of the people who were. As strange as that might sound, it goes to show that God is not limited by anything or anybody—and especially not by our sometimes narrow expectations of the way he works! He has always been an unpredictable player in human history.

Jethro sat in the entrance of Moses' tent, stroking his beard and watching thoughtfully the scene that had been unfolding before him for a few hours now. Moses had been sitting nearby since early morning with a queue of people waiting to see him . . . a queue that seemed to be getting longer rather than shorter. He was busy doing what Jethro often did as a Midianite priest—dealing with disputes about relationships, property, all the many other day-to-day issues which always arise when people live in community with one another. Jethro looked at Moses. He seemed to be enjoying himself, although he was clearly getting tired in the intense desert heat. Then he looked at the people in the queue. Some of them had been there for hours and were becoming increasingly agitated. And significantly, some of the people who were leaving the tent after receiving advice or direction from Moses were clearly unhappy with the help they had been given.

Jethro sighed. Still the same old Moses, he thought. Even after all those years he still had the tendency to act independently.

Later on, as the sun started to disappear behind Mount Sinai, the queue finally ended and Moses left the tent and walked wearily over to Jethro. Jethro cleared his throat and said, cautiously, 'What is this you are doing for the people? Why do you alone sit as judge, while all these people stand around you from morning to evening?' (Ex 18:14ff).

Moses looked at him in surprise. He had expected praise, not criticism, from the man he had been so eager to impress. 'Because the people come to me to seek God's will,' he said. 'Whenever they have a dispute it is brought to me and I decide between the parties and inform them of God's decrees and laws.'

Jethro thought for a moment and replied gently, 'What you are doing is not good. You and these people who come to you will only wear yourselves out. The work is too heavy for you; you cannot handle it alone. Listen now to me and I will give you some advice, and may God be with you.

'You must be the people's representative before God and bring their disputes to him. Teach them the decrees and laws and show them the way to live and the duties they are to perform. But select capable men from all the people—men who fear God, trustworthy men who hate dishonest gain—and appoint them as officials over thousands, hundreds, fifties and tens. Have them serve as judges for the people at all times, but have them bring every difficult case to you; the simple cases they can decide for themselves.

'That will make your load lighter, because they will share it with you. If you do this and God so commands, you will be able to stand the strain and all these people will go home satisfied.'

Moses gazed at Jethro in astonishment, his mind racing with what he had just heard. And once again he realised just how much he had to learn from this man whom history would scarcely mention . . . and how his training as a leader of God's people never seemed to stop.

Jethro could never have known it, but the advice he gave that day didn't just shape the administration of the Jewish nation. It set guidelines of organisation which have been used—and are still being used—in almost every country on earth! He helped to shape world history. They were principles which Jesus used when he fed the 5,000 and indeed, when he entrusted the work of taking the gospel to the whole of the earth to eleven frightened and somewhat unqualified disciples. And they were used by the early church when the apostles appointed deacons because they were getting overworked looking after God's people, as Moses was. It was advice that has stood the test of time.

There's an old saying that goes, 'It's better to set a thousand to work than to try to do the work of a thousand.' Growth can only be achieved by delegation. And delegation creates character—not just in the people doing the work, but in the people delegating it, too.

There are some vital elements within Jethro's advice which are worthy of particular attention.

Not all of it holds good for today

While most of Jethro's advice will help our modern churches to become happy and healthy, there is one aspect of it which should be resisted at all costs! The instruction 'You must be the people's representative before God' may have been appropriate for that period in history, but we should resist it at all costs now. Because of Jesus, the great High Priest, we are now *all* priests before God. We do not need men or women to represent us. There's nothing particularly new about this—the church has believed in the priesthood of all believers for centuries now. But it is still so easy for us to expect leaders to act as Old Testament-style priests—and leaders often still behave like them.

We need to remember that leaders don't have a special access to God on our behalf. We have equal status and equal rights of access to God's throne. Jesus died to establish it! So we should make sure we use it. We all need to remember that God himself is our shepherd, our counsellor, our teacher, our healer and our deliverer, and we should turn to him first in times of trouble. We should lift our eyes to God for our strength—not drain some poor leader who is probably on the brink of a breakdown himself because of the many demands upon him! That's not to say that we won't involve God's people in our lives as well. To fail to do this is fatal and is a quick way to deception! We must always remember that we are a body. But we need to take care that we don't create leadership structures which allow an Old Testament-style priesthood to creep into our churches.

Even as early as AD 95, church ministers were being referred to as High Priests, Priests and Levites, and the practice is always ready to rear its head today unless we take steps to avoid it! Like many kingdom truths, believing in the priesthood of believers is one thing. Actually living it is another!

Prevention is better than cure

Jethro didn't just tell Moses how to deal with disputes more effectively—he also told him how to prevent them, by teaching people God's decrees and laws, showing them the way to live and the duties they should perform. I am convinced that pastoral work in many churches would diminish if people were given regular teaching on these areas, since most of our problems emerge from ignorance about one or more of them.

Character versus gifting

Jethro was very clear about the kinds of people Moses was to delegate his work to. They had to fear God, be trustworthy and hate dishonest gain. It is important to note that his selection criteria all related to what they were like, not what they could do.

There is an emphasis today on raising leaders on the basis of their gifting. This is dangerous, because it can mean that the wrong people end up in positions of authority. The Jethro way is to appoint them on the basis of their character.

Jethro was also clear that the people being appointed as judges should be selected from all of the people. This is significant, too. It wasn't just the people who had relationships with Moses, or people whom he liked. It was *everyone*. Raising people into positions of responsibility purely on the basis of their relationship with the existing leader means that the leader will probably end up gathering a cliquey team of Yes men and women around him.

Pyramids belong to Egypt

Many people believe that Jethro was setting up a hierarchy or a pyramid of command that day. I disagree. This goes against the heart of God who sees all of his people as being equal, although with different functions. God's delegation should never produce a pecking order or an administrative chain of command to some elevated person or distant place. Jesus spoke strongly against this in Mark 10:35–45, when James and John came to him looking for some kind of elevated position. 'You know that those who are regarded as rulers of the Gentiles lord it over them, and their high officials exercise authority over them. *Not so with you*. Instead, whoever wants to become great among you must be your servant, and whoever wants to be first must be slave of all.'

Significantly, the system of hierarchical leadership came from Babylon, which Scripture uses to illustrate worldly practices. We see in Daniel 3 that King Nebuchadnezzar had a clearly defined system of satraps, prefects, governors, advisers, treasurers, judges, magistrates and officials.

Jethro was advocating a practical system of administration which still gave ordinary people access to Moses if they needed him—not a rigid pyramid or hierarchy. Moses left the pyramids behind him in Egypt. So should we.

The benefits were two-way

Jethro was clear—delegation brought benefits for everybody. Moses' burden would be lighter, and the people would go home satisfied. It was an arrangement by which everybody gained. Presumably the Jewish people who came to Moses were *not* going home satisfied because first, they had to wait ages to see him, and secondly, they sometimes received poor quality advice because he was so tired. Frustration must inevitably have crept in.

The same applies today. You often find significant levels of frustration in churches where responsibilities are not properly delegated.

God had the final say

Jethro was very emphatic on one point—God himself had to confirm that his advice was the best way forward. He stressed the fact to Moses twice. 'Listen now to me and I will give you some advice, and may *God be with you*,' he told Moses in Exodus 18:19. And he ended his guidelines with the words, '. . . if you do this, *and God so commands*.'

This is the hallmark of godly advice—it should always point people back to God. Jethro was careful not to dictate to Moses, because to do so would have been to have taken the place of God himself. We must be careful to follow his example, especially in churches today where people's submission to their leaders is actively taught and encouraged. The most that any of us can do when giving spiritual advice is to say what we think and what the Scriptures say—and then point the person back to God, as Jethro did.

And if the person rejects our advice after they've prayed about it, that is their right before God and we should give them the freedom to go their own way—even if we think they are wrong.

A leader's job is to convince, not to command. And it is very easy to convince people subtly, through a superior grasp of Scripture or simply by having a stronger, more charismatic personality. Giving people advice and helping them with their problems and disputes before God is one of the highest spiritual callings there is. It is what Jesus does for us now in his role as intercessor and great High Priest. We need to practise it like he does, with the greatest humility, gentleness and care. God never crosses people's wills, and neither should we. And we should be very careful before we tell someone that they are out of God's will because they are not following our advice. This is dangerous and unwise, because it can lead to us playing God. Ultimately, each person has to account to God himself for their lives—not to us.

Moses' chest heaved as he tried to control his tears. But he couldn't. They flowed and flowed. It had been hard enough to say goodbye to Jethro the last time, when he had departed on the mission to deliver the Israelites out of Egypt. But it was worse this time, for he knew, deep down, that he would never see his father-in-law again. Jethro was a very old man now and probably did not have many more years to live. And he was determined to go back and spend his remaining years with his own Midianite clan, apparently not the least tempted to remain with Moses and his daughter and grandchildren as they continued their great expedition with God into the Promised Land.

Moses hugged Jethro for a long time with one final embrace and then watched him walk off into the sand dunes. This time Jethro was not just walking out of his life. He was walking out of the pages of Scripture and into obscurity. How typical, leaving as unobtrusively as he arrived. He could not have made his exit in any other way. But the footprint he left in history remains.

Decades later, Moses took a decision that was perhaps one of the most difficult he ever faced. It happened just before he died, when God said to him, 'Treat the Midianites as your enemies and kill them, because they treated you as enemies when they deceived you' (Num 31:16).

So Moses took 1,000 men from each of Israel's twelve tribes and set out on one of the biggest bloodbaths recorded in the Old Testament. His troops eventually killed five Midianite kings and almost every Midianite man, woman and child in a chilling and merciless war.

We can only speculate about what was going through Moses' mind at the time. The Midianites were, of course, Jethro's people and were descendants of Abraham. And although Jethro had probably died by the time of the slaughter, maybe some of his descendants—Moses' in-laws—were among the victims. The mission cannot have been easy for Moses. And what would Zipporah have thought—her father's tribe being massacred at her husband's command?

One thing is for certain. Even though we are not required to act in such a military way now, obeying God in leadership is not for the faint-hearted.

The bulk of Moses' leadership training took place before he returned to Egypt to take responsibility for the Exodus. But he soon discovered, as we all do, that you never come to an end of God's training programme. It lasts until the day we die. And if we study the rest of Moses' life we can see some important principles which stood him in good stead and enabled him to go down as one of the greatest spiritual leaders of all times. We would all do well to learn from them.

He was willing to learn from others

We have already looked at the advice that Jethro gave Moses in Exodus 18. But the point which needs to be emphasised is that Moses acted on it.

We are told in Exodus 18:24, 'Moses listened to his father-in-law and did everything he said.' This is the hallmark of a good leader. He didn't try to defend his actions or save face. Quite the opposite, in fact—he recognised his failings and did something about them. And indeed, history tells us that Moses eventually went further with his powers of delegation than Jethro had originally suggested.

Jethro told him to select leaders *himself*. But later, in Deuteronomy 1:13, Moses says to the people of Israel, 'Choose some wise, understanding and respected men from each of your tribes and I will set them over you.' In other words he became secure enough to allow the people to choose their own leaders, rather than do it himself. This principle re-emerges in Acts 6, where the twelve apostles said, 'Brothers, choose seven men from among you . . .' And that's what happened: the brothers chose the deacons—not a practice you find in many churches nowadays. The apostles simply recognised them by praying for them and laying their hands on them (Acts 6:7).

So we can see that Moses was open to advice—and not only carried it out, but developed it, too.

He depended on God when it came to making difficult decisions

Moses' job of leading the people of Israel consisted mainly of dealing with one crisis after another. And on almost every occasion where there was a decision to be made, he went to God first. God virtually led him by the hand through the Red Sea and gave him clear instructions at every stage. Moses did not grow out of his total reliance on God until he was much older.

Moses ran into his first problem three days after leaving Egypt. The people were not able to drink the bitter water at Mara and complained. And although Moses was used to finding water in the desert after spending forty years there, he none the less cried out to God for a solution (Ex 17:4).

Moses was reliant on God. All good leaders should be— and should remain so. I always get nervous when I see a leader who is too confident and self-reliant. Perhaps God does too.

He had an intimate relationship with God

The hallmark of Moses' ministry was his intimate relationship with God. He ate with him, spent forty days up a mountain with him on two occasions, he seemed able to hear his voice with amazing ease and regularly met him face to face on a friendly basis in the tent of meeting (Ex 33:7–11). Of all the great leaders mentioned in Scripture, he stands alone in terms of his closeness with God. His relationship with him was so natural and so simple that it is an inspiration to all of us.

We need to follow his example and make sure that we are constantly developing our own intimacy with God, especially if we aspire to the privilege of leading God's people. We can only lead them to where we have been ourselves! And the problem is that if we possess natural leadership ability, we will find ourselves able to lead people quite easily with little attention to God—for a while. But it will always end in trouble. This is where Moses went wrong when he tried to set himself up as Israel's deliverer. He trusted in his own ability—but didn't have the relationship with God to complete the task successfully.

As leaders, our *intimacy* with God is far more important than our *ability*. And yet so many leadership courses concentrate on developing people's skills. Teaching them how to develop a closeness with God will serve them far better in the long run.

He was obedient to God

Moses soon found that the main principle of spiritual leadership is not so much leading people, as following God yourself—and then making sure the people come with you!

Moses' forty years as Israel's leader mainly consisted of following behind God, with the people following behind him. He either followed a pillar of cloud, a pillar of fire (Ex 13:20–22) or the Angel of the Lord (Ex 23:20–23).

The best way to judge a leader is to ask, 'Is God in front of them?' If he's not, we'd best not follow them, because if they are not following him then it will be unwise for us to follow them!

Epilogue

Mount Hermon towered above the hills, its blinding snow-capped summit twinkling and glistening in the sunlight more than 9,000 feet above the plains of the Jordan valley. The mountain did not have a peak . . . more a great arch, flecked and furrowed by different shades of light reflected by the snow from a thousand protrusions and dips. The air was sweet and crisp and the quietness intense, broken only by the cries of birds as they looped, dived and soared above the craggy slopes of the ancient volcano which was once a centre of Baal worship.

On one of the mountain's ascents, three men stood together, praying, away from the crowds, away from the pressures, away from their friends. After a while, something remarkable happened. One of the men changed. His face began to dazzle fluorescently like the sun and his clothes burst into a radiance more vivid than a silver flash of lightning or the majestic crown of the mountain itself. It was a breathtaking scene, charged with power and with the transcendent glory of God.

After a while another two figures appeared, they too

blazing in magnificent splendour. They began to talk to
the first man in one of the strangest and most remarkable
conversations in history . . . a conversation between Jesus,
the Son of God, Elijah, and Moses.

Hundreds of years had passed since Moses and Aaron
had led the people of Israel out of Egypt, through the Red
Sea and towards the Promised Land of Canaan. And after
putting up with his double-minded countrymen for forty
years in the wilderness, Moses died on the plains of Moab.
God buried him personally in the valley opposite Beth
Peor after a titanic dispute over his body between the
archangel Michael and the devil. The Israelites mourned
him for thirty days.

Before Moses died God took him to the summit of
Mount Nebo and showed him the Promised Land in all
its lush richness and splendour: Gilead, Dan, Naphtali,
Ephraim, Manessah, Judah as far as the western sea, the
Negev and the whole region from the Valley of Jericho, as
far as Zoar . . . the land of milk and honey.

But that's as far as Moses ever went into the land which
God had promised him. He saw it, but never entered it—
and it was his headstrong attitude that was to blame. One
day at Kadesh in the Desert of Zin, the Israelites ran out of
water and, as usual, rebelled against Moses and Aaron.
And Moses' angry response was to do what he'd done
before. He struck a rock to release water from inside it,
ignoring God's clear command to try something new and
speak to the rock instead. Moses' wineskins had grown
hard. He couldn't adapt to change. He became like many
churches, both denominational and newer ones, and stuck
to his safe areas. And his hastiness—that same hastiness
that caused him to murder an Egyptian eighty years
earlier—cost him the chance to lead his people from
Kadesh into Canaan. He had his successes, but never

really sorted out flaws in his character and so missed out on some of the bigger prizes that God had for him.

It was a high price to pay for a moment's rashness. And yet God was merciful. Despite Moses' disobedience, God allowed him into the Promised Land centuries later, at the transfiguration. And on the slopes of Mount Hermon Moses would have seen hundreds of square miles of fertile territory that had been eventually occupied by the Jews under Joshua's leadership. What a privilege—to stand with Jesus and Elijah and discuss Jesus' forthcoming execution with him . . . a privilege that surely more than made up for missing out on leading the Jews into Canaan himself.

Moses was in good company that day. Elijah, too, was a failure . . . a dynamic and yet depressive prophet who never really recovered from the spectacular successes of Mount Carmel and who spent much of the rest of his life in relative obscurity. And then, of course, there were the three disciples, Peter, James and John, asleep on the mountain to begin with and then terrified at what was going on, with Peter blurting out the ridiculous suggestion of building shelters for Jesus, Moses and Elijah to stay in.

Those five men are typical of everybody that God has ever used to fulfil his purposes. They had a heart to get it right, but never quite made it. They were human, just like you and me. Moses spent a lifetime being prepared for leadership by God, through different circumstances and people, and yet when the chips were down he still blew it. But because of his mercy, God got him to the mountain top in the end, just as he will with us. And when he does, we'll realise that it was his grace that led us there rather than any great achievement on our part. That will stop us from getting proud—and will help us to treat one another with mercy when we inevitably fail from time to time.

The call that God places on us is no different from the one that he placed upon Moses. Most of us can probably look back over the years and see how God has preserved us, prepared us and used adverse circumstances for our good, just as he did in Moses' life. And we all have both the capacity and the opportunity to make our impact on history, just as he did.

Who knows, some of us might even learn the lessons of obedience better than Moses did and actually inherit our Promised Land while we're still alive. What a challenge that presents to the thousands of us who are all leaders in the making!

Index of Life Issues